Trance

a collection of poems

in English, German and Turkish

hülya n. yılmaz

inner child press, ltd.

Credits

Author
hülya n. yılmaz

Editor
hülya n. yılmaz

Photographs
hülya n. yılmaz

Cover Art
Siddartha Beth Pierce

Proofing
Janet P. Caldwell

General Information

Trance

hülya n. yılmaz

1st Edition: 2013

Publisher Information

1st Edition: Inner Child Press:
intouch@innerchildpress.com
www.innerchildpress.com

LOC : 1-1069746381

ISBN-13 : 978-0615938790 (Inner Child Press, Ltd.)
ISBN-10 : 0615938795

$ 22.95

To Schlow Library,
with appreciation for its commitment to reading,

Hülya

Hülya N. Yılmaz

Hülya Yılmaz

April 8, 2014

Dedication

with my all-consuming love,

gratitude and in utmost respect and admiration . . .

I dedicate this book to you,

Bir Tanem, Gizem'im.

Thank you for giving me a life to live.

Acknowledgements

Hesna Ergün Yılmaz, my mother was one marvel of a human being. As my first and passionate reader and critic, she is the one who instilled in me the courage for and perseverance in creative writing during my early years. Who had the most recent impact on my written work to now see me arrive at this magical point in my life? Please follow me on my chronological thank you trip.

Cankardeşlerim – my heart's siblings have my eternal love and gratitude for having equipped me with the notion that my writing mattered, matters and will matter. You have stood by me through my most trying ordeals in increasing patience and understanding, reminding me with your eager love to keep sharpening my pencil for the healing. And I thank you for all you have done and continue to do for me.

I dared to make my first ever poem submission in English after becoming a proud member of a local writers' community – Nittany Valley Writers Network of State College, Pennsylvania (NVWN). My three poems – appearing in this book with proper credit – enjoyed their first publication *Pastiche*: *The magazine of the OLLI at Penn State Writers' Special Interest Group*. I thank you all, dear editors, not only for finding those poems worthy for public display but also for encouraging me to write more. Writers' Critique group – a branch of NVWN, a small circle of author friends with big accomplishments: I owe each and every one of you big! You, after all, had to endure a considerable number of my prose and poetry drafts – kindly trying to help me shed my native tongue's influence on English sentence formations. Thank you, Alan W. Jankowski, author of *I Often Wonder* – also by Inner Child Press, ltd. for your continued support and resourcefulness. I thank you, Elizabeth E. Castillo – author of *Seasons of Emotions*, for your graceful endorsement of my book. Crystal Schall – writer and editor: Thank you for embracing me from the first time we met despite my rather out-of-the norm communication traits.

For C. Hope Clark – author of the Carolina Slade mystery series as well as editor and founder of *Funds for Writers*, I have a different note of thanks. Behind her back...Her reach-out power in a NVWN workshop a few years back incited in me the importance of a blog site for one's writings. On the night of her seminar, mine emerged and I have been posting my written work with consistence since. I am humbled and honored to have a growing number of kind, caring and supportive but also forgiving author readers today. I am ever so thankful for their presence and support. In connection, I thank Hope – every time I log in to my site to post a writing.

Kathy Salloum – Public Relations Director, Advertising Manager and Creative Writer/Director, my dear friend: At a moment's notice, you gave so much of your time and loving attention to my poems' drafts. And you have done it all with such grace that I can't even begin to reciprocate. I am working on coining a unique term of appreciation to better articulate my thanks for you. Coming soon.

Then there is you, Dr. Kiriti Sengupta, dental surgeon and author of *The Unheard I, The Reciting Poets* and *My Glass of Wine*. You have been remarkable in your efforts to counter-balance my shyness in speaking about my own poetry. I am also most thankful to you for your passionate words of endorsement.

Dear Siddartha Beth Pierce – an artist, art historian and the author of *In the Beginning and the End* and *I Do*, I was thankful simply for having met you. But then came your astonishing artwork. My book's cover design. I thank you for helping me achieve completion for *Trance.*

As for you, the inspiring souls behind Inner Child Press, ltd. – a unique publishing enterprise with scholarships for unpublished authors: I learned about your existence only in recent times. I heavily fantasized after entering your Universal Poetry Month 2013 Essay Contest: About a home for my poetry with you. Witnessing your production of *Trance* – my first book of trilingual poems has been an utmost memorable experience for me. I often told you in our communication throughout, and I will repeat it again: My heart thanks you, author and poet William S. Peters Sr., the Founder, the Managing Director and Publisher of Inner Child Press and author and poet Janet P. Caldwell, the Chief Operating Officer of Inner Child Press. For letting my spirit move as it chose to and had the courage for on the way of my *Trance*'s fulfillment.

Preface

I was born to a small family and was loved very much as a child, youth and young adult. When on my own path, I imitated what I had learned from my mother and my father: I took responsibility for parenting. Of my inner child. But, unlike my parents, I neither acknowledged nor accepted it. Nor did I provide it with any loving – unlike what my parents had done with me. For decades, I lived aloof to the vital needs of that inner child to survive. I lived in a state of trance. Given my initial identity – my name, I thought such existence was intended for me. "Hülya," after all, translates in to such half-conscious state: dream; daydream.

I don't know how and when awareness settled. Numerous experiences within the third space where I have been breathing – somewhere between the Turko-Germanic-American existence, prompted transformations in me. Some were soul-shaking, others had a passing impact. My poems reflect the nuances for you and for me, such as "before her end" and "goodbye, mom" as opposed to "Loneliness"and "the backyard circus." As you will conclude, two states of being connect them all: love and melancholy. The same two human conditions always defined my persona. In *Trance,* I entrust my poetic narrations the immense responsibility of tending to my inner child's elations and miseres. The urge to listen to them now has a simple reason behind it: I chose to experience a trance-like state in the direction of life through them. As for the encouragement to voice them, it came from a most treasured friend – with the following words by the American poet, Mary Oliver (b. 1935): "Instructions for living a life: Pay attention. Be astonished. Tell about it."

My poems tell you about a life passed by me, at the same time – with their mere appearance in this book, they announce to you and me a life I decided to live. Whether their construct is in English, German or Turkish, I deeply hope you will recognize your own stories in them. However, I wish you will mostly relate to the poems of rejoice and not need to seek solace in those where I mirror deep sadnesses.

As for me, I have long ago made a lifetime commitment to love. Better yet, one was made for my inner child before birth. And, I am not done with melancholy as of yet, either. For it, too, was predetermined. I must be confusing you right now. Allow me to explain:

Hülya, a novel authored by Oğuz Özdeş (1920-1979) found my mom's hands during a very difficult time in her life. Though diagnostic procedures were quite limited, her mother was thought to have a sudden onset of ovarian cancer – her death ensued soon after. (Years later, the same cancer type was to claim my mother's life.) During my grandmother's illness, my mom had become pregnant with her second child – me. I never asked my mom why she read this romantic prose during her pregnancy. For *Hülya* is one of the saddest literary works I have ever encountered or used as a material for my teaching. The protagonist lives and dies in agony of her all-consuming love for a married man. It turned out that the period of my life soon after I first met my namesake book, marked itself for me as a time of one of my most tragic losses. Still, wherever I move to, whatever I give away or throw out, my personal copy is always with me. It was, after all, autographed by the author himself, solely for me – not because my name happened to be the same as his novel's title. It was, rather, because his nephew had back then just entered my life to become another most treasured friend.

From my precious belonging – the back of the third edition, I give you first in its original Turkish and then, in my own English translation *Hülya*'s synopsis by the author, whose memory is still utterly dear to me:

"Bu romanı okurken, hassas ve mustarip Hülya'ya muhabbetinizi, onun kaderine gözyaşlarınızı esirgemiyeceksiniz."

"While reading this novel, you are not going to deprive the sensitive and emotionally anguished Hülya of your love or of your tears for her fate."

Love and melancholy. Two traits that defined me throughout my life thusfar. Not very different from Oğuz Özdeş' Hülya – the young woman whose tragic love captivated my mother to the extent that she adopted her name for me. As I have said before, I have a commitment to love. When it comes to melancholy, I am considering a healing interaction with it – an initiative I have already prompted with my poems for *Trance*. I do intend to accomplish a continued healing, though. To begin to achieve such endeavor, I may have to write a different ending to Hülya but to hülya as well. And, I believe I will.

hülya

Foreword

I call her Dr. Hülya .

It was just recently during one of our banterous exchanges that i addressed her as such. Her education and institutional achievements do warrant her to be addressed as Doctor, however if you know her as i am so honored, you can not help but feel the warmth of her humanity and spirit shine through such containments.

Many *forewords* will indulge in critique of the body of work that lies before you. To some very finite degree i do as well, but i will not take the liberty of spoiling your journey as you wonder and wander through the ensuing verse laden pages and accompanying narratives.

hülya n. yılmaz is first and foremost an exemplary model of what i feel all human beings should be, caring and considerate. As i said earlier, she is warm, intimate and compassionate. She exudes her concerns for life, the people and circumstances that make this experience so grand.

In the following pages of this book you will experience the marvel of hülya n. yılmaz, the Human Being, hülya n. yılmaz, the Woman, the Mother, the Daughter, the Student and of course, the Teacher. She conveys all of these wonder-filled personages through her writing, not only in her Poetry, but within her carefully and insightfully worded narratives that accomplish various works.

This book, *Trance* is being offered to the world in three languages; English, Turkish and German, as denoted in its titling. Each of these tongues do have their own distinct romantic flavor and voice. As a Publisher i had no other choice but to consider the possibilities of what could be done to further the enchanting experience for the reader by way of exploiting the gifts of hülya's *Life Experiences* and Education. We made agreement to offer to the reader, not only the poetry, but the translations, for those such as myself who do not read nor comprehend to any significant degree, German or Turkish. I have teased her at times that this book, *Trance* allows her to again do what she does best . . . Give! I believe through her particular nurturing spirit and her attention to detail, that as a Teacher she is pretty damn effective. She most certainly is very thorough.

hülya's poetry exemplifies her courage to be honest and authentic as she shares her personal rectitude with the reader. In getting to know her, one realizes, that in her personal journey, she has collected many life metaphors, memories and lessons. She effortlessly shares these gems within her verse, thereby lending to each of us her reflections and contemplative examinations. Her subject matter though mostly about *Human Interaction*, can not easily be dismissed. You will not help but recognize a piece of your self sitting between the lines, wallowing betwixt the quiet expressive adjectives, the stirring adverbs and prepositional phrasing. In spite of her formal education, she writes from her heart, though her need and desire to instruct is ever present. I could say much more about this particular entity whom i affectionately call my friend, Dr. hülya, but, i will leave that for you to discover for your self as you take the voyage through the pages of Trance. In the following pages, you will touch hülya's humanity, and i pray you touch your own.

Enjoy

William S. Peters, Sr.

Inner Child Press

Table of Contents

Table of Contents ... *continued*

Table of Contents *... continued*

Table of Contents ... *continued*

Table of Contents . . . *continued*

Table of Contents ... *continued*

Table of Contents ... *continued*

hülya n. yılmaz

Trance

a collection of poems
in English, German and Turkish

hülya n. yılmaz

inner child press, ltd.

3/2/2007 8:44pm

My Poetic Perspectives

&

Voice

~ * ~

English

a few words from *hülya*

I was born and raised in Turkey, a country whose formal language is Turkish – a branch of the Ural-Altaic language family, together with Finnish, Estonian, Hungarian, Turkmen, Tatar and Mongolian. English is a foreign language I have acquired after German. My discovery of each, however, occurred within significant time intervals: I entered the German-speaking environment in my early childhood, whereas during my acquisition of English, I was an adult – a young one but still an adult.

Considering that my K-12, undergraduate and masters' degree schooling all took place in my country of birth, the literary voice you may have expected to hear from me would have to be "anadilim" ("my mother's tongue" – the English "native language"). Yet, *Trance* unites English, German and Turkish in order to enable for me three different literary voices, fulfilling their own unique roles and functions.

Why English?

While still living in Turkey, I took English classes from the American Language Institute in Ankara. That was in my early twenties. Being in the same family as German – my first acquired language, learning English seemed rather easy to me. It was at a beginners' level, though, where I had – according to my own standards – achieved proficiency before moving to the States. When I began my doctoral studies (in Germanic Languages and Literatures), the native-German professors were, as understandable, happy to hear me use the target language of the program.

Nevertheless, I did self-studying to advance upon my knowledge of and proficiency in English. With no formal classes. A fond memory comes to mind here. It was right after I received my acceptance letter from the doctoral program of the graduate school of my application. I knew I just had to get better with my English competence. I applied to the ESL program office in our area. Then, I met the person in charge of enrollments. My letter generated their interest, he told me. We began to communicate. In spoken English. A few minutes later, he paused, looked up and said – with a sweet smile: "Save your money, please. There surely is no need for you to take any classes with us!" For, I had no reason to think I could speak with him in any of the two languages I knew best, I had only the third at my service. English, thus became the language of my self-expression in public.

Poetry, then, demanded from me to use it also for its articulation.

I had become an expert at camouflage. My precocity allowed me, chameleonlike, to be to each what they required me to be.

The Power of One

Bryce Courtenay
(1933-2012)

the woman's place*

a beauty
eyes – green, almond-shaped
thick long lashes, distinctive brows
dark radiant hair – complexion, fair
slender, waist thin – long shapely legs
a fine boned petite
intelligent
confident
forthright
articulate
a mother of two
an alien in her home land

caution! they advised:
this, a tiny town
word gets around
women heed their household
not strut their being out loud,
dare talk as good as men,
or ever know to think more

she may have been a beauty, too
maybe also a mother of two
her still warm frame screamed her youth
not much was left of her disfigured face
marred, the rest
an alley kitchen's door – temporary home
under heaps of garbage refuse

a random incident! they said
the new teacher, the one out of town
who lived on, by and to her own

only then she saw the color of warning:
this, a tiny town
women heed their household
not strut their being out loud,
dare to talk as good as men,
or ever know to think more

~ * ~

*"the woman's place" is a poem inspired by noir and imitates the voice of a detective. An actual murder of a young woman had, however, taken place in an ultra conservative small town in Turkey where my father was serving as a veterinary doctor. Back then only a toddler, I heard their account of the incident many years later.

minds, contaminated*

female virginity
eternal purity
its lack: the primary taboo

before during after matrimony

timeless obsession
ageless restrain
tireless phobia

true loves chained
vibrant lives ruined

oh, my sweet home country
depossess your manhood already
conceive your women in whole
remember the wisdom they wore
countless centuries before
see the substance beyond the frame
stop being a fool of inordinate fame
make yourself a new name
the bodies are never the ones to blame

~ * ~

*In "minds contaminated," I touch upon a dilemma that causes suppression of world's women, not only in 'my sweet home country' – Turkey, an otherwise utmost beautiful corner on earth.

adapt

your mother, in bed to her death
aborting on your mind
lacked nourishment for the one inside

she lived

your hug warmed her a ring
tears uttered sadness in disguise

a premature bundle of bones
dark-haired body wrinkled
no contest to your first-born:
a striking baby boy
handsomely white from head to toe

yet your love was the same
with it though soon the dominance came

not that wear this, lend grace to your walk
feet in tight distance, not back and forth
arms on the side, in sync with the rest
harmonize

fine, a left-handed tote, if a must
adjust shoulder well – of course both
head up, relax neck

never inside the lids: liner outside
mascara on occasion, when required
skip color on the lips; omit the blush, too
hide acne, for sure; a powder stroke, or two

henna is a must! accent the eggplant hue
keep it long keep it loose, not below the waist!
apparent lack of height – no need to emphasize

he is the first ever, not to forget too young,
a bookish boy to boost; spoiled an only child
his mother over-demands; aunt too much of a socialite

stop meeting every day

…

mom, you know i have
although for each moment i crave
as i am anything but strong or brave

good willed but...*

we ate this girl's head*

no cannibalistic act

parental failure

~ * ~

*The first line ("Biz bu kızın başını yedik" in Turkish) is a regretful remark to or behind a child whose life quality parenting mistakes may have compromised.

love gone wrong (Pantun*)

often advice is given on self-respect

what though are each of the selves' conditions?

Is it feasible to uniformly expect

the tyranny of one fits all admonitions?

~ * ~

*Pantun is defined as a Malay poetic form with love being its most common theme, embodying an abab rhyme schemed quatrain with each line consisting of eight to twelve syllables. The claim is there may be a display of a semantical disconnect between the first and the second two lines, although a relation of some nature is evident.

raising a wife

his love, never fallen into her
evident to both for long
her hurtful honesty from the outset
then no longer
only at the end

no wasted effort on his part
all had to go along his way

yet, she, resolute
reared in full idiocy
brought up in static obedience
accommodating – except for the self
gratifying – except for the self

catering to him incessantly
catering to his household
catering to his profession
catering tirelessly
catering

his
ego
grew
more and more
just more and more

as
as were
as were such
as were such growth
as were such growth at all
as were such growth at all possible

one day she was no longer
body intact for sure
yet she was no longer
she was no
she was
she

Curse

1
"You'll find your demise!"

I have.
As has he.
Ahead of me.

I of selfless love.

Weak in breakage.

Was the innocent heart not already my demise?

I of selfless love.

2
She loves him.
Where, though, is the sun?
The water?
Air?

Blame is upon me.
Blame is always upon me.
My own curses do agree.

anatomy of a divorce*

onto death i want to lay the self
my One and Only's hope eyes erase the bed
before the head makes contact

onto death i want to lay the self
deadlock is all i feel
what have i become
what though had i been

the husband . . . former already
weary, distraught, ruined
my One and Only's sun face takes a shadow now and again

it all began with her inside me
love took off to eternity with her every smile
my only precious bond to life
for whom i pushed aside the self
not one small regret
the one for whose hope death does not get me today

i made us a home, i glorified it
on my own for long, too long of many years
filling in for all marital lack:
a promise is a promise after all!

years left, tens of years passed away
multiplied into trying decades
once looked aback, there exists a husband . . .
my One and Only's sun face takes a shadow now and again
her graceful not yet disheartened soul wound up
on the verge of a leap onto her own life
but . . . how about . . .

no, no, not possible!
once my One and Only is no longer home
having set onto her own path
the husband and i . . .
ways of ours ever so apart
how long, until where?
if the self can remain as self, that is!

onto death i want to lay the self
my One and Only's hope eyes erase the bed
before the head makes contact

onto death i want to lay the self
deadlock is all i feel
what have i become
what though had i been

~ * ~

* "anatomy of a divorce" has been previously published under the title "twinning with Munch" in *Pastiche, The magazine of the OLLI at Penn State Writers Special Interest Group*, Issue 5, Spring 2012.

a guide

All see it with ease

A rare gem of a daughter

He? The ego wins

~ * ~

*With this Haiku, I am re-visiting an issue very near to my heart – an occurrence often overlooked among parents: our children are a gift to us – a borrowed gift. They are their own persons, with their own feelings and thoughts, entitled to make their own choices. Unless anything about their life initiatives presents the risk of hurting them, we, as parents, owe them one feat: to treat them as we want or need to be treated by them.

imbalance

Loved? Şüphesiz!*

Cared for? Şüphesiz!

Respected? Şüphesiz!

A son's finances: hooked to a lifetime support.

The daughter somehow must breathe without.

*şüphesiz (a Turkish adverb in negation): "with no doubt." The poem articulates my subdued critique of patriarchal mentality – indiscriminative of any cultural entity.

why now ?

re-married
three hundred eighty four months long
half a sorrow year after his love of life

nerved aggressive insult-full
he's had it with her, now he concludes

the son the daughter-in-law
financed throughout their lives
a mere few blocks down
can't stay there…

besides…

desires to be on his own

with the daughter

in the midst of her life struggle
after prolonged decades
continents away

impossible!
too much resentment
if for nothing else…

One cannot step twice in the same river.

Heraclitus

(ca. 540 – ca. 480 BCD)

when love is everything*

among long-time friends once again
enduring the familiar left-side pain
decades surpassed their centuries
the hurt remains the same

an Immortal Beloved* crafted life
birthed death ever so keen
a blazing desire in-between

oh geh mit, geh mit*
oh accompany me, accompany me

Hebuterne* embraced the call
Plath* followed it with ease
Claudel* suffered a living disease

King Edward VIII* stunned the monarchy
etched to memory for lives to come:
the essence negates all that is told
nourishes from the authentic self;
sates and attains for evermore,
absolute ecstasy at the core.

For love is everything.

~ * ~

~ * ~

*Romantic love, to me, is an eternal state of being. As such it can only be conceived – nothing to explain or to describe. Staying true to my conviction, with this poem, I am merely pointing out love's impact on some of the most famous personalities and their lives.
*Immortal Beloved: A masterpiece created from love letters by Ludwig van Beethoven (an 18th century German composer and pianist). "oh geh mit, geh mit" are lines from the work with their English translations following in the next line.
*Jeanne Hébuterne: An early 20th century French artist who is known to have jumped to her death with her unborn child upon the death of her love – the Italian painter and sculptor Amedeo Modigliani.
*Sylvia Plath: A 20th century American writer of poetry and prose who is known to have committed suicide after losing the love of her husband – the English poet and children's writer Ted Hughes.
*Camille Claudel: A 20th century French sculptor and graphic artist who is claimed to have been committed to a mental institution for longer periods of time after her married love – the sculptor Auguste Rodin ended their relationship.
*King Edward VIII (1894-1972), the Duke of Windsor, has famously abdicated in order to wed Mrs. Wallis Simpson, who was married at the time.

memories on call again

an ordinary day
to class as decades before
time has since not been the same
nor remained unchanged the space

a campus nook
age-resistant couples

sweet tender hugs – everlasting
even temporary break up – hard to bear

head turns fast away
heart wishes to stay
bitter-sweet fossil tears hide
the smile attempting to grow inside

first love
shattered

barren no more

once a creek of bountiful flow
though lacking the dew the evening mist too
among the countless drying away

endured in abundance
snow-craving winters
rain-thirsty springs
long parched summers

yearning in solemn unease

a cloudburst then passed her impasse
through thick innumerable trees
amid myriads of blanketing streams
soaked one by one the bone-dry leaves

each of its caressing drop in gait
eased her drought of eternal wait

once obsessed

effort opens my eyes to a new morning
the old armchair of your fondness
stands alone pitiful sad lonely

in sight of my sorrow
even the sea bans its music
has demands from the blue clouds
commands they strip their vibrant dance
abandons those daring in cheer to commence

your first-time pleading eyes
your private invite in disguise…

my self-resentment never learned to set me free
self blames my alter ego in times of desperate misery

pathetic sense of innocence!
senseless pathos over purity!

evasion

the day fades anew
high moments and banalities recede
evening hours set in
hand in hand with that familiar pain

sadness rules

simple and intense:
i miss you
want you

yet you distance
detach
evade

i merely want your breath next to mine

perhaps…
just perhaps…
a little while longer

alive ?

body numb
mind on hold
voice in tremor
extremities, on ice
violent shaking
head spinning
air dried out

when will the eyes infer
ears finally heed…

how hot the blaze on the corpse?
how deep the gash in the heart?

postponing the self

waited
from the outset

dared to cite
a woman's invite to unite
an elite member of times long past
from the Empire of the Ottomans at last

the choice though had been made firm
no hope was left to affirm

waited
from the outset

this time it is the end
must stop wishing to further extent
for tomorrow's ills are yet to be met

How ?

I changed; they so tell me.
How can the before be without you?
I smile as if a cry; they so tell me.
How can bliss survive without you?

My vigor, long lost; they so tell me;
that I must try harder to revive myself.
The self is ripped from its sustenance.
How can there be life without you?

My youth is the hope; they so tell me;
that the pain will ease when older.
I am buried alive without you.
How can I endure time; they won't tell me!

wishing for

a call
a line
a sight
presence

to reminisce
exchange
interact
argue
part
settle
reunite
recompense caress
love with no end be loved

solo living for freedom for ease
its thorns oft long to displease

fictive mind

last night sleepless for my rare trip to a vacation
a popular television show attracted my full attention
a woman falls in love with a man: a couple quite becoming
his news reaches her before no return:
ex-girlfriend is expecting
he confesses in grave anguish
he must stand by the mother of his baby
five months for both are still ahead…maybe…
the inescapable force of all forces falls upon her
Eros had long ago chosen him for a custom-cast spell
"my heart will get broken," she knows –
"what if, though, it is all worth it?"

today on the road Sezen offered me her Turkish soul song
"I couldn't know I would hurt you by loving you so"
the agony of her love destined to be a no go

expectant and fulfilled arrival at my breathing space
i did not travel light for a three night room and board
put to shame the record of my ten-day case for abroad

my first night out
i put on a black sleeveless midi dress
threw over a blood orange whole-body shawl
heavy glimmer jewelry accompanied to impress
black open-toe shoes high-heeled quite décolleté
may have been in vain for a woman dining alone
as far as the judgments would wonder in stress

this soul ascertained to tell itself a different tale
it was there with you donning a smile of enormous scale
with each of the slow sips
its unending delectable wine
its mind dove deeper to a smooth rain-washed lake,
rather divine
it then devoured the immaculate sunset for two
before its inventive eyes

oh, by the way, it wasn't all black or blood orange on me
there too was something bright red inside...
my bleeding heart

the coward self

sorrow – sly – lurks near by
walls ring the primeval blame calls
not one sight no other sound
lungs choke in leap for healing breath
blood left the body far ahead

curses, you ceaseless thirst!
you cruelest yearning!
curses to you, you youless i!

born a half
loved less
destined to live as more

mourn in reproductive regret

love first

what color his room?

where his desk, favorite chair?

the embrace mattered

anguish

a new dawn breaks
seas join the infinity of mountains and dales
the agony of missing you
slithers, sobbing, in to me, and pales
a distinct whisper in the wind
lends me in pity our final breath
before it denounces my lifelong commitment
with no hope for a further fulfillment

leaving it to fantasy…

aching anew for his skin on mine
soft intense surprise-filled caress
yearning lips that never miss
the silkiest whisper of "yes?"
each time i utter his name

childlike smile in his eyes
in step with his handsome face
starting on those shapely feet
in invite to dance along with grace

wipes away my internal tears
appeases in faint promise to ease…

my love

doesn't long for another
for the beloved is in the breath
surrenders with zealous passion
as the beloved is as was once

doesn't force life onto death
while the beloved brings the breath
doesn't die with each passing day
as do those who with ease forget

is a promise from the core
defies time until skins decay
the beloved is found anew
however with a tragic delay

submits until the last breath
without pushing life to death
doesn't die day by day
while still taking in and out a breath

denial

gaps in comprehension
dryness in the throat
sense of paralysis
rapid heartbeat
the mouth, parched
memories' eyes, resolute
lungs gasp for air, stabs here and there

could never say goodbye

illusion ?

clad in yearning once again
several decades lived apart
unaged heart still seeks its twin
vindictive nights elapse in vain
soul's devotion surpasses the frame
relents unwilling in submission and pain

yet…

incessant the night – won't want to end
the day somehow won't want to ascend

clad in yearning once again
determined the memories – not one a waste

but…

has love indeed ever taken flight?
have two hearts pulsated as one?

a cry in red

don't be burning, oh heart, don't be yearning
for those who omit a love like yours
mistake dear life for a faithful gift
survive on dead commands adrift

refuse dismay, oh heart, reject despair
your fireball tears must promptly cease
you will not always be ablaze
one bright dawn will soon lend you a gaze

don't be burning, oh heart, don't be yearning
you loved at the core to self-annihilate
what difference does it all ever make
someday also this burn will abate

dying to life*

heart slows its beat
blood rushes to head
at every grasp of the loss
asleep awake
or in a dreaming state

ears deafen to sounds
eyes blind to colors
voice trembles steady tears
food serves to deaden the thirst

elation departs

eternal craving remains behind and keeps on and on

death comes
oh yes, it comes
but not to kill
condemns to life
the undying void inside

~ * ~

*"dying to life" has been previously published under the title of "Elegy – 3" in the September 2013 issue of the *Inner Child Magazine*.

I don't regret what I have lived,
My anger is possibly because of
what I haven't been able to…

Nazım Hikmet Ran
(1902-1963)

dis-ease*

today
gratitude stays away

"dis-ease" -
some instruct me to call it
those whom it does not visit
by no means "disease"!

twenty-four hours
year after year after year
constant companion

fatigue, aches, fatigue, pains, fatigue, disorientation, fatigue

work gets done
must make a living
at what cost?
triple the rest
to do only the least

reminiscing
Hannelore Kohl**
sun drains energy
body's defective demands

merely that

today
gratitude can stay away

~ * ~

~ * ~

*"dis-ease" has been previously published under the same title in *Pastiche, The magazine of the OLLI at Penn State Writers Special Interest Group*, Issue 6, Spring 2013.
*Hannelore Kohl (1933-2001), wife of former German Chancellor Helmut Kohl, suffered from a debilitating allergy to light.

~ * ~

the dead and the living*

my mother's grave, lost

too many look alikes since then

yet his dog finds his

*A 2012 news of a dog that wouldn't leave the grave of his owner for six years inspired me to write this poem. My mother who died of undetected ovarian cancer at the age of fourty-eight was buried in Istanbul, Turkey on a reserved family lot. Not being able to visit her grave is an ongoing emotional turmoil for me. Even if I were to live on her continent, I would be lost on that vast compound. Yet, this dog didn't and wouldn't.

cancer was more loyal*

Lilia, mein Schatz*
you won't know me
I left too soon

you were born of love and longing too strong
made me feel immortal by your side
merely a year though is all we had aside

a young woman you are now, no longer fragile
beautiful bright and loved very much
the precious darling in my arms back when
showering me with tiny beams of joy so immense
shaming even cancer of its ugly unwavering request

it is your birthday today
can't be there for you again this sorrowful mom
but don't be sad, mein Schatz, you are not alone
the one your eyes locked on in a time long past
a basement, my in-laws, on a cold summer night
when we both cradled your newly born delight
the one who perhaps mirrored me to you
for the color of her skin, hair and eyes' hue
whose both arms better secured you many a meal
before you glided to a sleep very deep and real
embraces you with both of our loves combined
whom I whispered to you in her mother's tongue
you know, mein Schatz, you met her online anew
the one who signs her e-mails hülya teyze* for me and you

~ * ~

~ * ~

* I wrote "cancer was more loyal" to honor the memory of my long-deceased cousin, Yasemin in my imagination of what she would have said to her daughter on any of her birthdays, had she not been robbed by a fatal cancer of any opportunity beyond a mere one year to celebrate her baby's much sought birth.

*mein Schatz (German): my treasure, often used as a nickname for a loved one

*Teyze (Turkish): maternal aunt but also an endeared non-biological aunt

primal pain*

no womb to take the tears to
the hurt above you –
only a petite full-grown
a premature fetal fist
forced to let it lurk
inside the three hundred ninety grams
as well the mere seven pounds
and not once not twice nor the nth time
but a content and eternal guest in you

*In its intent, "primal pain" is an apolitical writing, from line one to the end. Its imagery may, however, lead to wrong conclusions. My interest in composing this piece was of pure personal nature: immense emotional pain that led me to spiritual death – from which I came back. Again.

Sinopem*

the homeland enters the main vein
her scent floods to each body cell
one stunning aroma after another
i thirst in hunger pangs

etched to memory in blood and flesh
the magic of my early life
often asleep – head should feel sore
however when awake cold or ache no more
blanket soaking in her perfume
pillow, one of softest feathers
"snow falls upon who sleeps" she whispers…

one corner – a distinctive delight
a town in unison with its sea
unlocks the long suppressed

there!
it stretches to the harbor in cheer
main street down tea gardens of yesteryear
Divan café – loyal as ever before
hugs the aged salt factory to affectionately mend
guards before the old prison the compliant inner bay
not at all anxious by its fast descending bend
sates with secrets-devouring treats
my childhood eyes and arousing sighs
on loads and loads of mouth-watering plates
a huge piece of Revani* – apt for my sweet-tooth-fame
topped with natural ice cream of vanilla beans
delights generation after generation after generation
eight in total the loved ones of mine

farther away lies the town's aorta
the legendary passage to famed Ada
coveting April 23rd parades of ribbon bouquets
on Çocuk Bayramı – Festival of Children…
flows in sync with streets wide open alleys unseen
carries along a dear one of mine
to the heart's mind scene by scene

my eyes lock on the trail to the highest peak
one modest look to the left or the right
the sea struts its azure wealth and might

and there a breath away
dons mysteries that spectacular house
bricks worn out shutters ashen hue
still erect in humility though
vies few more breaths to accrue
ornate transoms eye the vastness of the sky
their weathered glances down upon the sea
the soil tender as a new mother's caress
depleted tree roots soon to finally rest
as have those who were put there abreast

my heart wanders off to the faded print:
wide steps to a wooden tall entry door
a stately man – fedora briefcase handsome face
my uncle by his leg – a mere toddler
a Shirley Temple though Turkish – my mother
her tiny gleaming face ever so bright
glued to the colossal front window

my grandmother's beauty in the dark
on her lap my other uncle – her youngest
his cruel damaged pre-natal heart
cut off too soon his contagious delight

next to me
the unique scent of my mother
the warmest warmth of her soul

~ * ~

*Sinop/e of the Turkish Black Sea – my adoptive birthplace –is the country's only peninsula. "Sinopem" is a self-coined wordplay for which I resorted to the Turkish possessive "m" suffix in order to hint at the reference "my Sinop" – as a possession of the poetic I. This small picturesque town is where seven generations on my mother side lived and died, where I, also will have my final home.
*Revani: A traditional Turkish dessert made of semolina and heavy syrup.

before her end*

two calls came – in sequence
heart depressed the potential pain
the swelling in her abdomen subsided
a surgery thus was scheduled again
not to worry standard procedure
but...if possible...to pay a visit...
soon

means were scarce – mere students
economy tickets sold out, visa for Turks rare
impossibilities when in a time bound
friends secured business travel
he of the German consulate opened Saturday doors
failed to note the name of his soul-filled eyes
would have thanked him with my life otherwise

seven and some hours on the plane

will she be in a stretcher
wheelchair perhaps – she is tough
to shorten the space between us
add hours to our remaining time

no sight of her at the airport...
two family friends alone
in the distance – far behind the security line
expressionless faces

the check-point officer tosses my passport
to a hit to the ground
as soon as its cover shouts to him my ethnic origin
succeeds to distract my anticipation of unbearable sorrow
until i am in the vicinity of my road companions

faint forced smiles in condescending hugs
one drives the other attempts to tell me gently...

my uncle – her brother and anesthesia specialist
her surgeon – a longtime acquaintance
along with assisting doctors
meet me outside for mundane pleasantries
with a large medical personnel entourage
i enter the hospital
the tallest, hesitant, whispers as if i were not there:
has she ever been...
hears his key colleague's confident reply:
no but my niece is utterly strong
too long of a corridor, quiet ice cold bare walls

her eyes when they see mine

her attack on all her life connections

her hands signaling to write

"I am dying. Let this end already!"

doctors activate the life machine anew
before the medications silence her with force
determined, she grabs another paper – pen was never let go

"Let this end already! I am dying."

heavy sedation
eleven days and a half

and i
just sat there
soundless soulless lifeless
allowed my traumatized senses spin me to a nothing

in her death-bed she was sounder than all of us combined

thirty-two years five months twenty-one days ago
her last breath exited her body
on the date her only surviving first family
her beloved brother
the anesthesiologist of her final two surgeries
had been born

~ * ~

*It is a tragic fact for me but nothing is a product of my imagination in this story-poem, "before her end".

goodbye, mom*

for the sake of saving me
both dear men succumbed to your iron will
a child's tale – one after another

oh, how i resented them

the growing abdomen before my wedding date
cancer's fast spreading rage
your sacrifice of your right to suffer

belittling was for you the end
a chiseled note a bare concrete
though on a vast family compound
intruders step on precious ground
laid in tears by generations abound

i haven't been there in too long of a while
i don't even think i want to find it
not an easy subject, that i know
an unfortunate taboo it was with you

your granddaughter is aware
she has courage
she is brave
her soul heard the ache in mine
tears of red did with ease define

i never had a chance for a goodbye
your granddaughter will escape that fate
hence the clause in my living will
her silent scream will not be as shrill

~ * ~

~ * ~

*Like "before her end," also "goodbye, mom," has no fictional element in it.

~ * ~

void

i put it in the full – didn't take it
i put it in the empty – didn't fill it

Turkish hence negotiates
"a dilemma of rather minor mess"
though this one is of grand magnitude
"i" picks this lore of folk nevertheless

this matter is one of lost identity
the claim is it reigned with dignity
knighted an "I" with distinction
a mere "i"? what a superstition!

when the wise asked why then…

the slap hit it hard, carved it to pieces
baffled the fragments of its tiny heart
it then thrust its "i" in grief aside
for it saw there never was an "I" inside

You need chaos in your soul
to give birth to a dancing star.

Friedrich Nietzsche
(1844-1900)

Loneliness*

"My loneliness is filled with people," Kafka

Loneliness once:
Nighttimes –the worst, amid winter darkness.
Days end in haste.
Day-ends prolong like childhood's gummy sweets
in the hands of street vendors, looking unkempt, unwashed,
lips not even touching the mom-water cup,
yet, devouring in full trust
those stretchy rainbow-colored sugar treats.

Loneliness now:
Filled with sounds of indecipherable joy
two person bed in the morning, two person bed at night
Quiet at nighttime but witness to a commotion at dawn…
The family of birds, greeting each new day
in non-stop frenzy
housed in my bedroom's right corner window crevice,
frantic back and forth wing-clapping
chirping
twitching
beak-to-wall-knocking
fighting off intruders.
How many birds were victims to slings
of childhood's neighborhood boys,
wood and ribbon killers of baby aviators
on their way to flying classes.

Loneliness now:
Filled with sounds of indecipherable joy.

~ * ~

~ * ~

*"Loneliness" has been previously published with the same title in *Pastiche, The magazine of the OLLI at Penn State Writers Special Interest Group*, Issue 6, Spring 2013.

the backyard circus

an outdoors person, i have never been
i despise crawling flying intruders on my side
but i refuse the snap of a hand or slap by a finger
so i stay inside – for my cute little actors don't abide

the squirrel feeder and its fancy servings
keep the small bird cafe in peaceful distance
humming wonder owns its own, for instance

all designed to have for each an orderly procession...
i have it here! no need for film or theater production

i take to my lazy chair in my living room to write
a loge corner, offers a cozy clear view to outside
i avoid the slightest beep, fear the storm window glass
will begin to tattle-tale my spy-like acts of high class

before i start i give outdoors a chance in a glance
and what do i see?

squirrels acrobat on at beneath the birds' territory,
although they glide
bunnies circle around near under an array of supplies,
won't abide
sparrows wrens peck whatever is left
on squirrel turf from before
a cardinal too large for the avian diner
pleads in a jagged shout
then flops its wings in a dance of grace
to a red forevermore
gangs of crows inch closer,
bully for a quick bite off snack

for a calmer spot opts the chipmunk
for it trusts me and my patio in full
it has known for long a secret fact:
my decorative pebbles mean a safe hide
and there never comes a sneaky mean strike

Tanka*

waiting on the dock

after a trying workday

warm, tranquil, sweet home...

fountains of impish waves

surprise! shouts a speeding boat

*A "Tanka" – akin to the American "cinquain" is a poem with a strict syllable pattern (5-7-5-7-7). The expectation is for the final two lines to introduce a surprising turn. The 2013 National Poetry Writing Month prompt inspired me to a poem. Then a video on YouTube, "Big Waves Takes Women by Surprise" practically wrote it for me.

Suffocation no more

A life of convenience. Beyond 4000 square feet.
Privileged. Secured. Drawn – his future's map.
Dark window covers.
Tinted windows.
Black shutters.

Then...

there is you
my love on you
your love and you
the skin-tight you

a gift nearby from afar
where the sun wakes up the sea
and the sea tucks in the sun

the yearning – unceasing…

yes, oh yes
the sun does set…
but it rises anew again

sole soul travel*

hours of road monotony
the GPS – self-imposed dictatorship
tired, bored, no more beauty in the snow

then…
a private gateway,
a much anticipated spectacle:
The Inn.
A compelling magnificence.
No need for a color, shade, or a hue;
a winter embrace of splendor;
the smolder of her fireplace…

I feel home.

Spacious beyond the eye's territory,
not at all an inn of limits;
high-risers' luxury at hand;
many may deem impersonal,
out of futile habit: This, a B&B?

I feel home.

Eloquent, the host – the hostess, of elegance.
The puppy acts like one yet outsizes me.
Struck by grave illness, the eldest feline
each night in my Victorian space.
She, too, will break hearts, never to replace the pieces.
Just like my Russian Blue, Duman.

A mere three days' span…
listening
inhaling
seeing
the authentic self
outside its tested and testing
fragmented, fragmenting
judged, judging
rushed, rushing
shell-self.

I am home.

~ * ~

*It was during one of my short break-away trips in the midst of a rather harsh winter that I discovered a magical soul-nourishing setting, a manor-sized Bed&Breakfast right on Chesapeake Bay. I wrote "sole soul travel" in the "Play It Again Sam" cafe in the nearby Chestertown. The revisions I made for *Trance* are minimal.

afresh*

splashes of light waves

hit the dry land on short loan

i revive again

~ * ~

*While I love to travel to discover new world beauties in people and landscape, I lack the time. My most favorite remedy to soothe my longing to escape life's monotonous ills is driving to nearby distances in the peak of winter – during my semester-break, as I have done before my poem "sole soul travel" existed. The Haiku "afresh" came about after my exhausted soul had a chance to revive itself in one of the most spectacular (if not the only one) Bed&Breakfast establishments in Bemus Point, NY.

grey*

"We write to taste life twice," Anais Nin*

glamorous empty wishes
drowning unknowns
vain convictions
nonstop doubts
tribulations

Black and white.

darkness of self-pity lifts
soul resolves to don scents galore
a dappled bouquet glazed in mirth
clears the canvas off ills though in uproar

at the stroke of the pen

grey emerges

~ * ~

*Anais Nin was a 20th century American author. Two of her most known works are *Delta of Venus* and *Little Birds.*

Bir Taneme*

with you
life embellished itself
laughter came strong
tears did stall
the sun found me
water began to run
air turned pure

i, however, burdened your light
once you no longer were a child
gave you many sad tears to shed
for you, my darling, they were not meant

you are forgiving, you understand
you even saw it all from my end

you are my sun
my water
my air

don't you ever despair
for this fortunate woman
loved pained and elated
lived all of life's beauties to bear

~ * ~

~ * ~

*"Bir Taneme" in Turkish translates as "To my one and only." My only child, a daughter, is what constitutes my life and love in its ultimate conception and materialization. The second stanza unravels an emotional suffering she has gone through and presents me – or any poetic I – as the one with all the responsibility for that past predicament. When, in fact, however, her tremendous hurt came about on account of a tragically mishandled divorce.

annenden*

my mother in grief over the fate of her own
feared i must leave before i came
my melancholy had thus been inborn
don't you ever think we four are the same!

i sorrowed after her in profound dismay
and the special two of whom you know
but also myself as it once was a whole

i of accidental life
a can* torn from its canan*

you of sought for breath
a dear canan to your can

set yourself to evade your ills
sail your heart to eternal bliss
life is stunning, as it is arduous
hurt is real, so are love's thrills

there will be an array of crossroads
keep on the paths you call your own
don't let a friend or foe confine you
whether with a mate or lover of value
lend esteem to a dost* through and through

~ * ~

~ * ~

*Writing a volumunous book about and for my daughter – an incredible human being – would be an easy task. She, however, is too modest to be in such a spotlight.
*annenden (Turkish): From your mother; can (Turkish): Life; soul; canan (Turkish): The beloved; dost (Persian-Urdu-Hindi-Turkish): Gender-neutral friend

~ * ~

Mourning for Innocence*

This time they were saved, the babies.
The killer, dead.
Timely.

Unlike the one who had aspired to live
for several rounds too many.

Oh, you innocent souls.
Sweet gifts of life. Future's treasures.
The present was stolen from you.
A mere one digit past yours was.

This stranger's heart refutes your final moments' terror.
Etches instead your enchanting smiles forever.

~ * ~

*When the Sandy Hook Elementary School shooting occurred on my birthday in 2012, I couldn't get my horrific scenarios-filled, imagined images out of my mind. When the pictures of the murdered children surfaced, I knew I had to write about them. Otherwise, their beautiful faces and the fact of their senselessly wasted and violently ended lives were going to keep breaking my heart again and again. "Mourning for Innocence" begins with a reference to the Quebec daycare shooting in 2013 during which armed attack – thankfully – no child was killed.

Elation*

bursting balloons wrapped in rainbow
carry the darkness up and away
splashes of refreshed, vivid colors
force the thunder clouds astray

arms wide extended, prancing to and from
myriads of rejoined, bracing town squares
shadows packed, locked, sent missing
more destruction, the storm no longer dares

frolicking wills move in instead
afar, nearby, nearing, or there
honed by the warmest, keenest of hearts
to soar over you, with utmost care.
Your new lives will not be bare.

~ * ~

*"Elation" has been published on July, 2013 under the same title in *Twist of Fate*, an international charity anthology by Indies In Action.

You Are Not Alone*

the skies may now appear as night
not much is left erect in sight
sorrow and destruction abound
whenever you look around

while despair may rise its ugly head
many cycles of sunshines still await
as in the hearts of those who here pen
these lines of care and encouragement

you don't know us, and we, not you
through our minds, though, we unite
with these words, we do embrace
all together what you have to face
you will, thus, begin a promising phase
inside a new home you will soon call your place.

~ * ~

*Like "Elation," "You Are Not Alone" has also been published on July, 2013 in *Twist of Fate*, an international charity anthology by Indies In Action.

a rare gratitude*

we mourn those killed whether by nature or human hands
are often quick to form groups of support
join in the pain in any way we can
honor collaborate reach out

yet
we forget
in the face of the ease
amid traffic on electronic space
who gave us the chance to compensate
for the tremendous loss of any violent decease?

the reporting souls for whom we tend to beget
outbursts of thunder fire but also twister effect
for we frequently resent
the tongue the style in their accounts
no further consideration we lend:
they are the ones we shall neglect!

there has been twice a ferocious whirling wind
uprooting helpless humans, many deceased

none though remained a mere number

there were infinite mourners
joined by precious young life
one of whom was amazed to face
how the living chose to commemorate
their dead in warm circles of those alive
greeted hope for new lives in full embrace

destruction and loss was vast in extent
volunteers of numerous count fast went

we onlookers non-locals
akin souls of continents called alien
were able to mediate in penning our appeal

for we have learned of your sorrow
from thankless efforts of journalism
professed by those who exist far and wide
who have not let your acute ills and needs slide

~ * ~

* Inspiration for "a rare gratitude" came to me from the discrete substance numerous journalists delivered during and after the horrifying May and June 2013 tornado hits in Oklahoma, U.S. During the time, an array of poets and writers from various parts of the world - as I have – were working on our contributions to create the charity anthology, *Twist of Fate* by Indies In Action – now a published book.

headlines: as good as it gets ?

world

Afghan children killed by Nato...
10 children and two women...
air strike...

UK urges calm over N Korea crisis...
despite the paranoid rhetoric emanating from Pyongyang...

Cairo clashes Coptic funerals...
of four Coptic Christians...
killed in sectarian violence...

Kerry warns Iran time is limited...
on its nuclear programme...
U.S. delays missile test over tension with North Korea...

the U.S.

new recruits combat sexual assault in the Air Force...
the first gun in America...

a mere scan reading –
violence war
war violence
more war more violence

Kansas Set To Enact Law
Saying Life Starts At Fertilization...

what if...
we were to first acknowledge
life in those already been born?

no !*

grave despair

ailment-laden days lacking means
career a dead-end labor-rich post
private life made believe

the alternative?
his sole question…

you loved twice they have gone their ways
sole stronghold your mother no longer
brother wedded father remarried

he worried…

on a pedestal same as the brother
they would know the best

she resolved

forced aside the heart's un-yearning
stayed on and on and on

until the rope of old teachings
sprang back where she had left a blank

inhaled
exhaled

exhaled again
again and again

lived

in euphoria

on the path of the spirit – the authentic one
freed once again from post-natal melancholy
in a triumphant attempt to pre-empt
the resolve of

grave despair

~ * ~

*A 2013 NaPoWriMo, National Poetry Writing Month prompt gave me the inspiration to write "grave despair" in the literary technique called "in medias res" – beginning and ending with the same word. From that starting point, with the help of information in Encyclopedia Britannica, I made the attempt to adopt the corresponding narrative technique instead. In sum, one immediately delves in to a situation critical in or for life, exposes previously occurred events as flashbacks and later develops the exposed.

final nostalgia*

rainbows repleting
splashed by the waves of my daily walks
soul out of its cage in ecstasy prances in trance along
my shadow, secured, seeks a reunion once more
still spry in high heels my frolicking essence
soars over the town square inside its sea
honed by the keenest of primal senses
awaits a vision in ultimate plea

~ * ~

*The object of my primordial yearning in "final nostalgia" is, once again the peninsular Turkish town, Sinop.

German

~ * ~

a language acquired

all German Poetry is followed by translation into English.

10:04am

a few words from hülya

The earliest memory I have of Germany has a view from the shoulders of my father. With passers-by looking at me with smiles. The next is "eine grosse Tafel Milchschokolade" (a large bar of milk chocolate) right under my nose, with my tiny hands protecting a big and thick slice of powder-sugared cake from being taken away from me (I am sure there is an ownership certificate for the term "sweet tooth" with my name on it somewhere.) As an old photograph from the family album told me several summers ago, my father's house still guards that picture. I became a matter of wonder with my dark and semi-curly hair and dark brown eyes – my parents and their witness German or non-German friends used to narrate to everyone back in Turkey. That was before the work migration of large groups of Turks to Germany in 1961; hence, before the country had begun to struggle with the integration or assimilation of its largest minority population.

I don't know whether it was that early childhood exposure to the German language enticing me to study it many years later. It could have been during the other times when my family and I traveled to Germany to accompany my father while he did his veterinary research. What I know is how fascinated I had become with the brand new sounds way back then when I was that little girl. But more so as the years went by, with my family and myself having spent more time in the German land, while my father continued with his research projects. Back in Turkey, I selected German as my foreign language option in middle school and high school and made a commitment to advance my knowledge of it in any opportunity I could get.

That determination took me through a bachelor's and master's degree in German philology and a doctoral degree in Germanic Literatures and Languages.

Since 1977, I have been teaching college students either the German language, literature or culture. In sum, the language of Germany has been largely my means of communication on the professional level. While the surface fact may be so, for my own pleasure, I have at times resorted to German also to write poems. I want to hope the pleasure will not be only mine as you read through them in their first-ever publications.

As for my German-to-English translations, I hope I have attained more losses than additions. For I remain of the same conviction the following words by the German poet and philosopher, Karl Wilhelm Friedrich Schlegel (1772-1829) uncover with specific regard to the essence of the translation process:

"What is lost in the good or excellent translation is precisely the best."

6/2/2008 7:42am

identitåt, die ursprüngliche

Bir Tanem* weiss es
sowie jede meiner herzensschwestern
treuester bruder in İzmir*, dem malerischen ort der türken
der autorenkreis, fürsorglich – aus der cyberwelt
die immer mehr wachsende dankbare lernkraftgruppe
meiner ewigen lehrvergangenheit wie auch von heute
die hoffnung meiner liebe, der hingebungsvollen…
den umfang meiner dankesschuld
für deren bestellung von glück
alleinig mir zuliebe

der name, jedoch, der mir gegeben
hat scharf das gegenteil zu vertreten
beweis dafür bin ich es doch selber
sowohl mein mehrere jahrzehnt langes leben…

*Bir Tanem (Turkish): my one and only
*İzmir: A historically most significant city in Turkey, situated on the Aegean sea.

identity, the original one*

my One and Only is aware
as is each of my heart's sisters,
the most loyal brother in İzmir –
on that picturesque site of the Turks
the caring circle of authors –
of cyberspace
the evermore growing group of thankful learners
of my eternal teaching past, of today as well
the hope of my love – the devoted one...

of the extent the debt of my gratitude
for their ordering of luck
only for my sake

the name, however, the one chosen for me
speaks sharply of quite the contrary
i am proof for it, after all
as is my multiple decade long life...

*I am herewith referring to the story behind my name, as I detailed it somewhat in the Preface.

geheimnis

hölle auf erden
gewöhnlicher spruch
keine ausnahme, dieses ich
wo es hatte sein zuhause

es war das ende
das absolute ende
wieso wurde es zu einer tragödie

das ur-ich fand sich dort
in einer einzigen rose
rot – knallrot
und erwachte mit mut

zu einem hohen augenblick…

ihre seele
die ermordete
springt heute noch von der stadtmitte in die meerestiefe
und ruht

secret

hell on earth
goes a common saying
this i had no immunity
where it was at home

it was the end
the absolute end
unknown, why it turned to a tragedy

the primordial i found itself there
in one single rose
red – bright red
and awoke in courage

to a high moment…

her soul
the murdered one
leaps still from the town center in to the depth of the sea
and rests

mutter

das öftere alleinsein
vor und nach der geburt
sowie seit früher kindheit
wâhrend mancherlei krankheit

horror-drehbuch im kopfe
treuer pessimist
in ewiger panik
angst um ihr kind
das einzige das wunderschöne das unglaublich liebe

sie låsst die sonne scheinen
entsperrt die urwasserquelle
füllt das dunkle mit hellstem licht
löst los den tod in reinste luft, ganz schlicht

kein baby verlangt es – nur wir allein
sicher ist sie weder dein noch mein
jedoch hast auch du
verantwortungen mit mir gemein

the mother

alone – a frequent occurrence
before and after delivery
often in her early childhood
for various illnesses, as well

in thoughts of horror-film plots
a loyal pessimist
in unending panic
fearing for her child
the only one, the lovely one, the amazingly dear one

she makes the sun shine
unblocks water's primal source
fills the dark with the brightest light
boldly, eliminates death to purest air

no baby demands it – only we do
it is certain: she is neither yours nor mine
yet you, too, are accountable
for the same responsibilities as i

litanei

litany spielt sie heute noch
als ob in seiner gegenwart

sie? halb? nicht mehr!
dank dem ersten treffen
nach dem unvergånglichen abschied
eins mit ihrem ganzen wesen!
das lange nur eine hålfte gewesen

litany spielt sie heute noch
als ob in seiner gegenwart

dennoch sah sie schwerleidend ein
wir gehören uns nicht mehr
hat sie es nicht verdient unsere zeitlose liebe
die überzeugung in seiner sanften stimme

tag und nacht dachte sie nach
in einsamen erbarmungslos langen
trostlos dunklen stunden
leidenschaftlich liebkosung verlangend
wie dann…

verteufelt human!
verpfuschtes leben!
wieviel långer muss sie noch leiden
sich von diesem leiden zu scheiden?
wann ist's genug?
wann ist's getan?

litany spielt sie heute noch
als ob in seiner gegenwart

was aber schmerzvoller...

der verdacht, der grauenhaft grausame verdacht

seine stimme gegenwart wie auch seine liebe

all dies sei nur…

litany

she plays litany still today
as were she with him

she? half? not anymore!
after the first encounter
ensuing eternity's farewell
united with her essence!
for long, a half

she plays litany still today
as were she with him

in agony, nevertheless, her realization:
we no longer belong together
didn't our timeless love earn it?
the convinced tone in his gentle voice

day and night, she reflected
in lonesome hours
long with no mercy
desolately dark
his passionate reach for a caress
how then…

cursedly humane!
messed up life!
how much longer must she suffer
to severe herself from this agony?
when is it enough?
when will it be over?

she plays litany today still
as were she with him

what, though, pains more, is…

the suspicion, the atrocious gruesome suspicion

his voice his presence his love as well

may have been all…

das zweite ich

unerwartet trat er in meine gegenwart hinein
bruchstücke atmeten noch im alten dasein
wie sonst dominierte måchtig der schein…

jedoch schmerzte es im innersten heftig
ein schrilles geschrei war dauerhaft dabei
weinte in heftiger trauer mit leid und wut
zum feind wurde atem sowie überlebensmut

aus dem gedåchtnis fiel er ihr eine weile aus
sein liebes wesen erschien aber ungeahnt wieder
seine feine seele trug sie zurück zum leben über
das herz wachte endlich auf, als gelangte es zuhaus

wo es auch in höchster euphorie ist heim geblieben

wie er sie verstand…ohne eines gleichen

wiedertreffen von zwillingsseelen
sollte denen nicht zugrunde gehen!

lautete ihr innerster wunsch

hoffnung, unbeugsam, blieb ihr noch lange treu
seine schöne ansicht wiederum zu erleben
für ihn durch ihn unsterblich zu leben

wenn aber sie nun ist mit sich allein
betrauern trånen den ersatzlosen verlust
unverhofft gelang ihr dieses kostbare geschenk
schaffte leider fort den letzten hauch aus ihrer brust

alter ego

surprising her, he entered life
fragments were still alive in her old self
in appearance, she was fine…

yet the pain inside was immense
a sharp scream lived in permanence
cried in fierce mourning in rage and agony
breath, a foe just like the courage to survive

his lovely being left her attention a while
then, appeared once again – nothing foreseen
his dignified soul carried her over, back to life
her heart awoke at last, as were it at home

and it remained there in highest ecstasy

how he understood her…no equal

a re-encounter of twin souls
should not perish!

chimed her innermost wish

unrelenting, hope stayed by for long
to re-attain his lovely sight
of eternal life for and through him

when she, however, is now alone
for the loss of the irreplaceable, tears mourn
this precious gift had come to her when not expected
alas! from her chest the final breath it depleted

auf kosten von...

abrupt
erzwungen
ohne weiteres

verzweifelt verwüstet vernichtet
erniedrigung unvermeidbar
selbstrespekt verstorben
gewaltige trauer
ohne trost

zu spåt… zu erwarten oder zu hoffen
was vor jahren war einst erwiesen...

nun
nur ein ich
ohne namen

at the expense of…

in haste
compelled
without warning

broken-hearted devastated destroyed
humiliation – inevitable
self-respect – deceased
daunting mourning
with no consolation

too late… to expect or to hope
what once was proven years ago…

now
a mere i
innominate

liebe (Pantun*)

sie entstand aus emotionen allein
ihr wesen und leben ihm zu widmen bereit
er war vornehm gebildet und sehr fein
es scheint, ihm glich ihre liebe der unfreiheit

~ * ~

*The full definition of "Pantun" appears under my poem in English, titled "love gone wrong (Pantun)". To avoid an annoying repetition, I also refer to it under my upcoming Pantun poem in Turkish.

love (Pantun)*

she evolved solely from emotions
her being and life poised for devotion to him
he was distinguished sophisticated and dignified
it seems her love equaled bondage for him

*In my English translation of the original, I do not conform to Pantun's requirements. It wasn't my intent to do so.

anhånglichkeit

statt abhångigkeit

des wesens bedarf an freiheit

seelennahrung sowie fürs alltagsleben

das leiden zu überleben
der entfernten körpernåhe

bedingungslos zu lieben

danke für diese gabe das teilen deiner weisheit dich

devotedness

in place of dependency

the need of the essence to be free

nectar for the soul, for daily life as well

to survive the suffering
of the body's distanced immediacy

to love without reserve…

thank you for this gift
for sharing of your wisdom
for you

es war einmal…

mann und frau
ringfrei

anziehung
respekt
vertrauen
verståndnis

gelangen zu ihrer heimat

und wenn sie nicht gestorben ist

lebte sie allein bis zum ende ihrer zeit…

once upon a time

a man and a woman
ringfree

attraction
trust
respect
understanding

arrived at their home

and if she did not die

she lived on her own until the end of her time…

egos

knochen und fleisch
nase, mund und ohren
und all das andere organ
im åusseren oder inneren
wozu
die erbårmliche übernahme von superioritåt?
die banale vorstellung vom klassenunterschied?

zu schade!

die eifrig erstellten bücher scheitern
belehren nicht das vollkommen offenbare

geburt tod
zeichnet niemanden aus
das leben ist ausserdem auch anderen zuhaus

egos

bones and flesh
nose mouth and ears
and all those other organs
inside or in the exterior
what for, the pathetic assumption of superiority?
the facile notion of class divide?

what a pity!

the eagerly compiled books do fail
don't teach the perfectly obvious

birth death
don't distinguish between anyone
life, moreover, is home also to others

zeit

heute und gestern
mögen in der zukunft erscheinen
und enthalten sich wohl im vergangenen

T.S. Eliot* - nach seinen worten

sicher erläutert er viel mehr
ich aber verstehe alles nicht so sehr
also imitiere ich unverschämt geschwind
eins aus meinem einstigen wissenswind
von Hans Jakob Christoffel von Grimmelshausen*
Simplicissimus Teutsch* - seinen berühmten
doch bloss um seines opportunen namens willen

simplizistisch müssen mir letzten endes eben
komplexe konzepte beigebracht werden
denn auf dieser komplizierten erden
gibt es ganz und gar viel zu viel zu lernen

was an mir jedoch scheint oft zu fehlen
begrenzt sich nicht unbedingt zur intelligenz
vielmehr liegt es an dem mir unverständlichen vergehen
nämlich an der zeit und ihrer beständigen präsenz

~ * ~

*Thomas Stearns Eliot: A 20th century American poet, essayist and playwright.
*Hans Jakob Christoffel von Grimmelshausen: A 17th century German author; Simplicissimus Teutsch, a novel is his most famous work.

time

today and yesterday
may be appearing in the future
and probably are present in the past

according to words by T.S. Eliot

he surely illuminates much more
i, however, don't get it all quite well
so: brazen-faced i imitate apace
from my lore's gust erstwhile
the famous Simplicissimus Teutsch
of Hans Jakob Christoffel von Grimmelshausen
but only for his opportune name's sake

it is in simplistic terms, after all,
how you must teach me concepts of complexity
'cause there just is much too much to learn
in this world of much uncertainty

what, though, seems to be often missing in me
is not necessarily confined to the intellect
it rather lies in a misdeed of my incomprehension
namely, time and its presence with determination

ihr baby*

einen wundernamen hat er zurecht
an hoffnung gross, erfüllt von bedeutung
den eltern steht zu die köstliche meldung

wenn allein jubele ich in der stille
übermütig erhebt sich meine seele
lange begleitete mich weder musik noch tanz
nun laden mich ein töne von himmlischer eleganz

dennoch fållen mich aufs reale leben
mehrfache sorgen um seine mutter
wie wird er seine geburt wohl pflegen

nach allem wåchst er in einem baby…

in dem meinen

*When I was working on the semi-final stages of *Trance*, my daughter – pregnant with her first child, had been preparing for her son's birth. She was in her ninth month. Knowing that my book's publication couldn't possibly precede the arrival of her baby, hence any potential for her to read anything from my book, I wanted to give her a surprise with this poem. I use the German possessive pronoun "ihr" (her and their) with purpose, as it suggests a reference not only to my daughter but also to her and her husband together. At the same time, I hint at a second female present – in the disguise of the poetic i.

her baby

he has a miracle name, and rightly so
big in hopes, full of significance
to the parents belong the news so exquisite

when alone i rejoice in silence
my soul, carefree, soars
lacked for long a companion in music
now ask me out tunes of heavenly elegance

nevertheless, many worries about his mother
fell me to the ground of reality
in what way will he administer his birth

he is, after all, growing inside a baby…

my own

my native voice

~ * ~

Turkish

all Turkish Poetry is followed by translation into English.

a few words from hülya

"We seldom realize, for example that our most private thoughts and emotions are not actually our own. For we think in terms of languages and images which we did not invent, but which were given to us by our society."

Alan Wilson Watts (1915-1973)

The words above by the British philosopher and writer prompted my initial deliberations on what appears next: Some of my "most private thoughts and emotions" in Turkish – my native tongue. To resound Watts, I "did not invent" this language or the "images" that enhance and enrich it. Nonetheless, writing through the voice with which I first perceived our world, is a gift of intimacy that sates a higher yearning for me. May it be in their original compositions or in my English translations of them, the poems in this part of my book will uncover for you that native voice. Hence, as it is my hope, it will help me achieve a deeper connection between us.

Throughout the previous sections of *Trance*, I invited you to some of the hardest ordeals I have gone through and expect to meet still. Yet, many other verses opened themselves up to you in their joyous sounds and imagery with a touch of brighter anticipations. Whatever tone my life experiences demanded from the form, content and imagery, all those verses related them to you in loyal devotion to authentic representation. The poems I compiled under "my native voice" are no exception.

Remaining in the hope for one day to be able to achieve a "complete poem," I would like to reiterate the insight Robert Frost (1874-1963) granted us all as my concluding reflections on "my native voice":

~ * ~

A poem begins with a lump in the throat; a homesickness or a lovesickness. It is a reaching-out toward expression; an effort to find fulfillment. A complete poem is one where an emotion has found its thought and the thought has found words.

Notre Dame'ın Kamburu*

Yağmur fütursuzca ıssız mahalleleri dansa çağırıyordu.
Bir karaltı çıktı gecenin ücrasından eksik ve sırtı bükük.
Kanatsız bir kuşcasına acizdi hareketleriyle etrafına.
Doğuştan olmalıydı tariflenemez bu kamburu.

Önce boş sonra dolan caddelerden geçti
ürkekçe topallayarak.
Her adımı bir çift tiksinti nefret dolu bakışla karşılanarak
omzunun yamuk yuvasına sığınan başına
tükürükler yağarak
hızla çemberleşen kalabalık dolu ara sokaklardan korkarak
insafsız sözde insan kitlesinden
boşuna kaçmaya çalışıyordu.
Merhamete susuz gözlerini
aczinden zevklenenlere çevirerek
sırtını gittikçe yoklaşan özüne çaresizce bindirerek
çarpık ağzında sessize yakın bir yakarış,
sağlam dizini yere bıraktı.

Son anına varmış bir idamlık gibi anlaşılmaz bir jestle
gözleri dönmüşlere tuhaf bir tebessüm sunuyordu.
Hakaret dolu iğrenç haksız suçlamalar bıçak gölgelerinde
az gelişmiş beyninde bir işkence silsilesine dönüyordu.
Çırpınmaya kıvranmaya başladı, yalvarmaya yeltenerek
fakat kurtulmaya küçük bir ümit bile veremiyordu.

Kulaklarına yapıştı insan dışı sesini bir haykırışa iterek.
Daha fazla direnmesine imkan olmadığını anlıyordu.
Olduğu yere yıkılıp kaldı son bir titreyişle irkilerek
Yaşamıyordu artık
Notre Dame'ın bir parça sevgiye hasret Kamburu.

~ * ~

* With "Notre Dame'ın Kamburu," I give you my earliest attempt at a theme where I am not the protagonist. This poem also stands out with its external format, as I had finally succeeded in constructing run-on lines - a desired element in formal spoken and written Turkish. As for the inspiration, it came to me from the same-titled novel I had read for the first time while a sophomore in high school. Especially, after I saw a musical production of the work, my fascination with Quasimodo's tragic love story and fate kept growing. Then, my imagination took off, to the point to have him die by choice – of heartbreak. The image of the knives serves to represent hatred.

The Hunchback of Notre Dame

The rain was indifferent in its call for a dance
to desolate neighborhoods.
A silhouette, incomplete, his back curved, emerged
from the loneliness of the night.
His movements were feeble, as if a wingless bird.
His indescribable hunchback had to be inborn.

Fearfully, he limped through the empty streets
they were now getting full.
Disgusted hatred-filled looks confronted each step
spittles poured on his head
he tried to shelter it in his crooked neck
scared, attempted in vain to escape
from the relentless crowd, supposedly human
through side streets,
now filled with people encircling him.
In thirst for mercy, he turned his eyes
to those delighted by his weakness
hopeless, he lowered his back
in to his body, disappearing so fast
a silent prayer in his askew mouth,
he fell on his good knee.

As if under a death sentence, in a strange gesture,
to those enraged he gave an awkward smile.
Under the shadows of knives,
insult companions, disgusting accusations
echoed as tortures inside his weak brain.

With an attempt to beg, he convulsed and writhed.
He had no hope to escape.

Shouting an inhuman scream, he covered his ears.
He knew not to fight it anymore.
In one last shudder, he fell back.
Together with his quest for a little love,
the life of the Hunchback of Notre Dame had just expired.

Yavrundan Sana*

Yağmur yağarsa dışarıda, gözyaşlarım sanıyorum.
Ağlayan bir ses varsa, senin sesine benzetiyorum.
Veda eden bir yüz görsem, senin yüzünü buluyorum.
Ruhum bir an daralsa, senin ruhunu hatırlıyorum.

Ufukta bir karaltı belirse, onda hemen seni tanıyorum.
Neden mi? Bilemem ki anne!
Didinen, uğraşan bir kadın görsem şekil değiştiriyor birden.
Annelerin kraliçesi, benim annem oluyor aniden.
Nedimelerin de her biri üstelik ayrı bir kraliçe, anne!

Sensizliğimi bir an hatırlasam, nankörce
Artık gözlerim buğulanmıyor anne.
Nasıl ki, öyle tasavvur edemiyorum seni de
Ağlamayı bırak, sihrimiz kaybolabilir anne!

~ * ~

*The poem, an acrostic in its Turkish version – repeated in its title, came about during my junior year at Erenköy Kız Lisesi in Istanbul, Turkey – a boarding school back then. Staying away from my family was my own choice, for I didn't want to lose a year of my studies while my father completed a research project in Germany. The tone behind my native voice best evidences how I missed my mom.

From Your Offspring To You

Whenever it rains, my tears! is what I can think.
If I hear someone in weeps, I take them to belong to you.
A face at a farewell brings along yours to me in haste.
Where my soul chokes, your spirit is already there.

A silhouette appearing in the horizon
fast resembles you.
Why? I don't know, mom!
A laboring woman in struggle
transforms before my eyes suddenly.
She becomes the queen of all mothers,
rapidly mirroring your image.
And, each royal maid is herself a queen, mom!

In your absence now, mom, ungratefully,
my eyes tend to run out of water.
My wish is for you to also be sob-free:
stop your cries, mom, for our magic's sake!

ebeveyn sevgisi

doğmak onların sayesinde
büyümek ise aynı şekilde
yaşlanmak bir şans eseri
kaçınılmaz bir olgu iş ölmeye gelince

peki, ya yaşamak?

biz biz miyiz
onların yansıması mı yoksa?

diyelim ki, sevdik
hem de çok sevdik
uymadı ama o onların hülyasına*
demek ki, bir olamayız artık o sinecanla

fakat zaman sabırsız ırmak
katmış önüne nice yaşamları
coşmuş köpür köpür yudumluyor
bir ruh bir beden bir sevgi
onun şiddeti karşısında ne farkeder ki

canan artık bir başka canın yanında
kalmış diğer can yitene dek tek bir başına
kavurur ruhu bedeni derininden bir yanık
sönmemiş sevgi özlemle birbirlerine tanık

işte ömür! bitti bitiyor
hayat sadece bir kez gelip geçiyor

yanlış anlaşılmasın
çok sevildik, çok da sevdik
kendimizce düşünmek nedir
onu hiç bir zaman öğrenemedik

~ * ~

*I am making a wordplay in the original language but it unfortunately gets lost in the English translation: He was no fit (1) either, for their dream ("hülya" in Turkish) or (2) for their daughter named hülya. Also important to know is the use for "can" and "canan," in classical Turkish literature, in particular: "can" means "life" but also "the essence of a human being," namely "heart". "Canan," a proper name when capitalized, means "sweetheart; beloved" – in the sense of romantic love, as I have intended it for this poem.

parental love*

to be born – thanks to them
growing up, the same
to age – a matter of luck
when it comes to death: unavoidable

how about living?

are we ourselves
or, their mere extension?

let's say, we fell in love
and loved to extremity
he, however, didn't meet their dream*
in sum, then: the heart's mate's chance is none

yet, time is an impatient river,
has for long put infinite lives at its feet,
it gushes, devouring them sip by sip
what does one soul one body one love matter
in the face of its force

the sweetheart now has joined another
as for the other heart, all alone until its end
a deep burn chars the soul ignites the body
unquenched fire and desire, witnesses for each other

here it is! life! about to be over
comes only once and passes

there should be no misunderstandings:
loved, we surely were
and loved back in return
though never able to learn
to think by and for ourselves

~ * ~

*Under the poem in Turkish, I am sharing a critical insight as to my wordplay with the meaning of "hülya."

Sinecan*

Yağmur sesi ile uykum bölündü bir gece birden.
Kağıda düşen gözyaşlarını andırıyordu damlalar.
Arada bir parlayan şimşek gürleyen yıldırım
bir insan sesiydi sanki için için hıçkıran.

Ruhu deşen bir çağrı vardı bu haykırışta.
Deniz dağ kara haşmetle göz önüne seriliyordu.
Tutulmamış sözlerin umut yeminlerini anlatırcasına
istikrar ve cüretle isyan dalgalı inip yükseliyordu.

Birden durdu ölümcül bir darbeyle noktalanırcasına.

Yaşantılar kendilerine döndü tüm aciz gerçekleriyle.
Ölüme can veren o muhteşem can hayal artık yoktu.
Koştum baktım dışarıya bir son ümitli ümitsizlikle.
Yağmur meğerse hiç yağmamış ve hala da yağmıyordu.

*The night I wrote “Sinecan” is a vivid memory. It was past midnight. I couldn’t sleep; I got up, turned on the swan-neck light on my small desk and began to experiment with words. Ankara was under a heavy rain attack. I opened my balcony curtains. The tall apartment building sitting now right in front of my childhood home wasn’t there then. Nor had my parents yet covered the balcony with metal-framed glass windows from its concrete up. In other words, I had a full open view to the outside. The sound of thick water drops against the glass captivated me. I can’t recall anymore when I went to bed. Before I did, though, my poem was finished. The poem’s title is a noun compound I made up using “sine” (bosom, breast or heart) and “can” (life; heart), in order to express the heart’s twin.

Heart's Twin

The rain's sound interrupted sleep one night.
The drops reminded me of tears falling on paper.
The thunderbolt and occasional flashes of lightening
resembled a human voice entwined in bitter sobs.

This soul-piercing cry had a hint of invite.
Sublime, sea mountain earth appeared before the eye.
As were they to tell of hopeful oaths of promises unkept.
In steady waves and bold revolt,
the weep was fading away to rise again.

It suddenly ceased, as were there a fatal jolt to end it.

Joined by their helpless realities,
lives returned to their before.
That heart's vision, once livened death, no longer was.
In one last hopeful self-despair,
I raced and looked outside.
Rain, it seemed, never was.
Nor was it now being.

Pişmanlık*

Sahiller boyu sürükleniyorum
boşa bir arzuyla seni görmek için.
Anıları çıkarıp tek tek göz atıyorum
elimde elini yeniden hissedebilmek için.
Bulutların o pek cömert insafına sığınıyorum
benden beni kaç kez alan iç alevimi gölgelemek için.
Bir kez daha seninle seni bizle beraber bulmak istiyorum
unutulma bezginliğinin gazap kaplı derisini
soyup atmak için.
O zamanki bizden izli ıslak kumlara haykırmak istiyorum
bugünkü yaşamların nasırlaşmış yordamından
beni ayırabilmen için.

Oysaki sadece…
bendeki sensiz boşluğa yoldaşım yasımı
tutmaya devam edebiliyorum.

~ * ~

"Pişmanlık" had been published in Issue 1 of *Resimli Roman* – a back then popular magazine in Turkey on December 29, 1975 in the "Şiir Köşesi", the Poetry Corner. The version here displays a dramatic revision.

Regret

I drag myself along the beaches
with desire to see you, in vain;
one by one, take out the memories,
to feel in mine your hand again;
seek shelter under the clouds' bountiful mercy
to lend the fire inside a shade,
the same one that tears me off of myself.
Together with you one more time, I want to find us
to shed my wrath-covered skin,
the same weary one, the forgotten;
I want to scream to the sands,
wet with our traces of the past,
to help you set me apart
from calloused habits
from today's lives.

Alas! I merely manage my mourning,
a steady companion of the post-you void inside.

Sensiz Ben

Gene sabah.

Gözlerim açılıyor güçlükle
bilirlermiş gibi karşıyı boş bulacağımı.
Antika koltuğumu benimsediğin o köşe
tokatlıyor bana bir kez daha yalnızlığımı.

Her yer karanlık.

Kara bulutlar çökmüş gök yüzü üstüne.
Bezmiş terketmiş o güzelim maviliğini.
Vermiyor biteviye alıyor benden hasetle
bendeki senin beni terketmez şefkatini.

Hafızamın bakışlarına dalıyorum hevesle
görürmüş tutabilirmiş gibi o eşsiz seninkileri.
Sarılıyor kucaklıyor inliyorum yitmez hasretle.
Kızıl gözyaşlarım adeta bulabilecekmiş gibi seni

I, without you

Morning dawns again.

Heavy, half closed my eyes
they know, it will remain empty what I see across.
The tiny corner with the antique seat of your embrace
slaps me one more time with my loneliness.

Darkness is everywhere.

Black clouds have now settled atop the sky.
Weary, it forsook its bountiful blue.
In envy for your tenderness, it eats away ceaselessly
the one thing of you not abandoning me.

Eager, I dive to my memory's eyes,
to seek a hold of those unequal yours.
I hug them, curl with them, then moan in unending yen
as if my tears of red ever could find you.

Avutmaca*

Değişmişim, bana öyle diyorlar.
Başka nasıl olabilirim, soruyorum, sensiz?
Gülüşlerim eksikmiş yüzümden, hayretle izliyorlar.
Tebessüm iplerim sende teslim, nasıl gülerim ki sensiz?

Boş boş dolaşıyormuşum, sorguya çekiyorlar.
Nasıl yeniden dolabilirim ki, soruyorum, sensiz?
Canlılığımı yitirmişim, dirilmemi istiyorlar.
Kalbim evsiz barksız, nasıl yaşarım sensiz?

Üzülmemeliymişim, benden gayret bekliyorlar.
Nasıl çabalarım mutluluğa, soruyorum, sensiz?
Çok senem varmış önümde, teselli ediyorlar.
Yüzyılların yükünü nasıl aşarım sensiz?

Belki de bana geri gelirmişsin, inanmaz, müjdeliyorlar.
Kalbim nasıl dayanacak yeniden atmaya,
soruyorum, sensiz?
Bezmemeliymişim, zaman yaraları sarar diyorlar.
Her nefesimde akan kanı neyle sararım sensiz?

~ * ~

*"Avutmaca" is one of my poems with which I come closest to "How?" with my emotional state. The inspiration of both was the same: Love after its loss.

Consolation

I have changed, I'm told.
I ask: How can I be different?
I am without you.
Lacking its smiles, my face is a surprise.
The strings are entrusted with you. How can I smile?
I am without you.

I walk around with no aim. I'm questioned.
I ask: How can I have a purpose?
I am without you.
My liveliness has withered. I'm required to resuscitate.
I ask: My heart is left homeless. How can I live?
I am without you.

I should not deplore, I'm expected to make an effort.
I ask: How can I strive for happiness?
I am without you.
Many years are ahead of me, I'm being comforted.
I ask: How can I defeat the burden of centuries?
I am without you.

I'm heralded: the word, though incredulous, is,
you may come back to me.
I ask: How can my heart survive beating again?
I am without you.
I am not supposed to grow weary of life, I'm told,
time will heal.
I ask:
How can I nurse the blood that floods with each breath?
I am without you.

Sen Yoksun

Yalnızlığımın kafesinden sana doğru uzanıyorum.
Yakarışlarım cevapsız kalıyor,
çünkü sen yoksun.

Kabuslu uykularımda uzanıp seni kucaklıyorum.
Kollarım boşluğa düşüyor,
çünkü sen yoksun.

Altı uçurum tek kayamdaymışcasına direniyorum.
Ellerimden tutup çeken olmuyor,
çünkü sen yoksun.

Anlağımın almadığı bilinmezlerde savrularak koşuyorum.
Kaybolmuşluğumu avutan olmuyor,
çünkü sen yoksun.

Zaman zaman zayıf bir umuda kanarak gülmek istiyorum.
Tebessümüm dudaklarımda donuyor,
çünkü sen yoksun.

Yer yer biraz olsun zehir akıtmaya ağlamak istiyorum.
Alev çağlayanlı gözyaşlarımı silen olmuyor,
çünkü sen yoksun.

Çoğu zaman dünyanın sınavlarına direnebilmek istiyorum.
Bel bağlayacağım kimse kalmıyor,
çünkü sen yoksun.

Gene de ümitsiz ümitlerde ümit dolu bir yoldaş arıyorum.
Ama bana hiç biri yanaşamıyor,
çünkü sen yoksun.

Yinelediğim biz ayrıcalıklı anılara dalıyorum.
Yasımdan bezgin her biri, kıpırdanmıyor,
çünkü sen yoksun.

Yüreğimde fosilleşmiş sitem ve şikayetler duyuyorum.
Yaşama gücüm beni hızla terkediyor,
çünkü sen yoksun.

Soruyorlar bir de bana, yaşam nedir diye, susuyorum.
İçim boş laf etmekten bunalmış, beziyor,
çünkü sen yoksun.

Bir gün sanki mühürlenmiş bir vahadan fışkırıyorum.
Son bir can çekişle korum sönüp nihayet yitiyor.

Çünkü sen yoksun.

For You Are Not There

I reach for you from the cage of my loneliness.
My pleas remain unanswered.
For you are not there.

In my nightmared sleeps, my arms extend and
embrace you.
They fall to emptiness.
For you are not there.

I hold out, as if on the only rock atop an abyssed cliff.
No one pulls me up.
For you are not there.

Scattered, I flow with the unknown, I can't comprehend.
No one comforts me whenever I wonder.
For you are not there.

Now and again, a laugh steals a faint hope.
My smile, frozen, falls on my lips.
For you are not there.

At times, a cry tries to stream away the ills.
No one wipes my fiery tears.
For you are not there.

I attempt to withstand world's trials.
There remains no one I can rely on.
For you are not there.

Still, I seek a hope-filled companion in hopeless hopes.
But, none can approach me.
For you are not there.

I renew and sink into memories privileged with us.
Each, wearier than my mourning, is motionless.
For you are not there.

I hear reproaches, grievances, all fossilized in my heart.
My inner strength leaves me swiftly.
For you are not there.

Having the nerve, they ask me: What is life.
I keep silent.
Suffocating from inane talk,
I am tired of living.
For you are not there.

One day, I erupt,
as though from an oasis, dried up for long.
In final agony, my ember burns out, and withers at last.

For you are not there.

Ümitsizlik*

Seviyor, yarınsız seviyorsun
yaşamı ondan* nefeslercesine.

Seviliyor, doymayasıya seviliyorsun
daimi bir tek sen var olabilecekcesine.

Tadıyor, sarhoşça tadıyorsun,
yudum yudum ellerinden içercesine.

Tattırıyor, şuursuzca tattırıyorsun
hayatın nektarını* çözebilecekcesine.

Ürküyor, kendinden ürküyorsun
olabilecek en ağır bir suç işlemişçesine.

Ürkütüyor, halinle ürkütüyorsun
yaşamış olmakla beddua hak edercesine.

Unutuluyor, muhakkak unutuluyorsun
aşk adeta hiç yaşama geçmemişçesine.

Sorguluyor, kendini sorguluyorsun
mahkemede sanık sandalyesindeymişçesine.

Sürükleniyor, kurumuş, kırılgan sürükleniyorsun
attığın hatalı adımların sekmelerinde ezilmişçesine.

Algılıyor, tek bir görüntüyü algılıyorsun
dipdiri sevgisiyle karşına gelivermişcesine.

Bakıyor, ışıksız gözlerinde umutla bakıyorsun
onun hala parlak gülümser bakışlarını görmemezcesine.

Sarsılıyor, kendini bırakmakla hiçleniyorsun
gözbebeklerindekine eş simsiyahların
önceliğine tükenircesine.

Çabalıyor, yatalak zihninle çabalayıp duruyorsun
ümitsizliklere sönmüş ruhunu lanetlercesine.
Bir son yanıkla yanındakine döndüğünü gözlüyorsun.

O meçhul sol köşende bitercesine
şuursuzca dalıyor, dalıyor, dalıyorsun
söndürür ateşini belki artık engin sular, diye
yitirdiğinden beri yerini dolduramadığın o eşsiz şefkatle...

~ * ~

"Ümitsizlik" had been previously published in Turkey by a back then alive magazine, *Resimli Roman* on March 25, 1974 under the title "Dolunay". The version here is significantly revised. Important to note is the Turkish "o" – a gender-neutral pronoun, and its simultaneous reference to "she, he, it" in English. In my translation, I opted to represent a male with it. As for "nektar," I apply it in the mythological sense; in other words, as the drink of gods.

Despair

You love, love without a tomorrow,
as were you to attain your breath from him.

You get loved, loved insatiably,
as were you to become the only one, eternally.

You taste, taste in a drunken state,
as were you to consume it from his hands, drop by drop.

You have him taste it, taste it senselessly,
as were you capable to decipher the nectar of life.

You dread, dread yourself,
as were you one of a serious crime.

You appal, appal with your behavior,
as were you deserving of a curse, for having lived.

You get forgotten, certainly forgotten,
as were love never alive.

You question, question yourself,
as were you in court, as the accused.

You drag on, wasted, fragile, drag on and on,
as were you crushed under each of your flawed steps.

You pick out, pick out only one image,
as were he right before you, the might of his love as well.

You watch, watch with hope in your darkened eyes,
as were his smiling eyes, still aflame, not a true sight.

You shatter, dissolve for having let yourself go,
as were you consumed by the sole attention he pays
to the black eyes, a match only to his.

You struggle, struggle on with your bed-ridden mind,
as were you to curse your soul to abate in despair.
In one last burn, you see him turn to his companion.

As were you to end the one on your left side,
you dive, dive and dive senselessly;
in belief the vast waters will quench your blaze
with the same unequal care
its loss you could never replace nor bear…

Kasvet

Uzaklardasın boynu bükük.
Anıların birer parça sönmez alev.
Kahrolasıya duygusallığın bölük pörçük.
Kendine bağımlı bir zulüm en yakın dostun

Olmazlıklarından şüphe duymadığın umutların
ona rağmen seni coşturabilen kendini avutmaların
çekmiş gitmişler görmüşler sende olmayacak bir yaratık.
Diyemiyorsun ki bir türlü geçmişe ağlamak pek boş artık.

Vardın romanlarından birine düşlediğin o noktaya.
Pes etmeyen ruhun kalan son hayat ışığın olmuş.
Üzerinde kat kat kimseyi ödünlemez bir toprak.
Haykırıyorsun doğuşunun sesini tanımayarak.
Boşuna bir gayretle bedeninden kaçarak.

Geçmişe ağlamak pek boş artık.

Gloom

Humbled, you are enstranged.
Each of your memories, a piece of undying blaze.
Your grieving sentimentality, in bits.
A co-dependent cruelty, your closest friend.

The hopes you have convinced to fail,
your ability to self-console for occasional elation,
have all left, seeing in you a living thing not to be;
for you can't seem to say: too late to cry for the past.

You reached the point you dreamt for one of your novels.
Your unyielding soul is now your last light of life.
Under layers of unrelenting earth you scream,
with the unrecognizable voice of your birth.
Fleeing from your body, in an attempt in vain.

It is too late to cry for the past.

Anneler ve kızları*

Rüyamda gördüm gene seni.
Hıçkırıklarım bile bozamadı sihrini.
Yalnız değildin bu sefer, yavrunu da düşledim;
uyandığında minicik bedenine bir tek beni istedi.
Giydirdim. Altını temizledim. Güldürdüm.
Oynadım bebeciğinle,
kendiminkiymiş gibi sevdim, kokladım, okşadım onu.
Ellerim an an seninkilerine dönüştü;
sendedir şimdi onun sıcaklığı, mis kokusu.

Nedense belirsiz bir yerde kalmayı yeğledin…

Senin yerine ben tattım, o miniciğinden özlemini.
Merak etme, iyi bakılacak yavruna;
sırdaşım, kardeşim, sen yeter ki kal huzurda.
Bul orada senden çok erken çalınanı burada.

Arada bir sorarsın herhalde annemin hatırını;
bilirsin seni çok, pek çok severdi.
Acaba neden önce beni istetmedi?

Götür ona yavrusundan en son haberleri,
üzülmesin, sadece huzur verenleri.
Bitmedim, tükenmedim henüz;
hala küçük bir yavrum var benim de ne de olsa.
O eşsiz varlıklarınızı yaşıyorum elden geldiğince,
kendi yavruma yansıtmak dileğince;
tanıtasıya sizin ender ruhunuzu onun benliğine.

Bilmem gücüm ya da ömrüm yetecek mi?
Bir tarafta sen, bir tarafta annem.
Kızım ve kızın ise yanıbaşımda…
Tamamlamaya çalışırken yarım özlemlerinizi,
unutmadan yavrunu da yavrumu da;
hem de doğru aktararak onlara sizleri,
hak edebilecek miyim acaba eşsizliklerinizi?

Meğerse iki melek yoldaşmış hep yanımda.
Yavruları burada, beraber biricik yavrumla.
Sığınıyorum güçlerine, güç geçmesi için bana.

Öylesine zor ki aslında,
sürdürmek efsanelerini arkalarından,
bir kez içtikten sonra
muhteşem hayat suyunu onlarla dolan.

Biliyorum...
anladım biraz
görevim şu ki:
yaşam amansız zorluklarla da dolsa
birçok zaman da umutlarım kırılsa
iç yorgunluklarıyla debelense ruhum
yaşantılar hüzün ve matemle sonuçlansa,
onlarsız onların tadını vermek yavrularımıza.

~ * ~

*I wrote "Anneler ve kızları" after one of my saddest losses to death. As some of my several other poems show, the extent to which I was experiencing the internal pain once again took me to writing. This time, cancer had just claimed too many dear ones too soon.

Mothers and their daughters

I had a dream of you again.
Even my sobs couldn't break your spell.
You were not alone this time. I also dreamt of your baby:
after her nap, she asked only for me.
I dressed her. Changed her diapers. Made her laugh.
I played with her, as were she my own.
I pampered, caressed and smelled her.
Time and again, my hands became yours;
her warmth, her heavenly scent must now be on you.

Somehow, you preferred to stay somewhere unknown…

I tasted the fruition of your longing for your baby.
Don't worry; your little one will receive good care;
My confidante, my sister, you just be in peace.
Find the one who was taken far too early from here.

You will ask my mom, how she is, will you not?
On my behalf? You know how much she loved you.
I wonder, why she didn't ask for me first?

Fill her in with the latest news on her little one,
but only the comforting ones, she should not be sad.
It is not over with me yet. I have not expired;
A young child of mine needs me still, after all.
I am living your incomparable beings,
to the best that I can,
to reflect you on to my own offspring;
to teach her soul your essences, so rare.

I don't know. Will my life suffice?
There is you, there is then my mother, too.
My daughter and yours are right here…
I wonder. Will I ever be worth it to be
the one to represent in accuracy,
to deservedly model for them
your unequaled selves;
while not neglecting your baby or mine,
while trying to bring to closure
your departures left behind?

Two angels, it seems, were my companions all along.
Their offsprings are here, together with my only one.
In my sobs on their shoulders, I seek their strength.

It, however, is an immensely difficult feat
to revive their legacies in their absences,
when one tasted a sip from the elixir
they once had filled.

I know…
I understand it somewhat.
It is my duty
to somehow feed our babies with their flavors without them
even though cruel challenges may have filled we call life
even though my spirit may have often been broken
even though my soul's fatique may struggle from its core
even though we know life ends on mourning and sorrow…

Sınanmak*

Ne yapmalı, bilinecek gibi değil bazen!

Nefeslenecekken zorlu bir koşudan sonra;
bir ağır yük daha şu hastalıklı zayıf omuzlara.

Bazen yeni gün karşılanmaya güç bekliyor sil baştan;
güneşe hasret bırakılıyor çoğu insan çoğu zaman.

Hele bir de çökmüyor mu o zor çekilir ağırlıklar,
hiç ara vermeden şu bedenin üstüne, zaten baştan kırılgan.

Her ne kadar bitiş çizgisinde de olsa feri sönmüş o gözler,
nefes bekliyor gene de her taze gün başlangıcından,
benlik yepyeni bir acıyı göğüslemeye mecburlanmadan.

Anlamaya çabalıyorum ben de, herkes gibi, bu bilinsin
çözmeye sırrını ezelden olagelmiş onca çözümsüzlüklerin.

Neden bu bitmeyesiye acımasızlık, diye diye
sitemler ederek sürekli tazelenen üzüntü çemberine.

İnançlı olsam soracağım: hiç bilmedin mi ki
tahammüllülüğümü, sana özentimi ve de sevgimi
çocukluğumdaki o ilk özümün seslerini.
Uzun zamandır hakim bana şüphelerim.
Eğer ondansa cömert acı çektirilmelerim.
Onlar aklın mutsuzluklu serserilikleri.
Şükret anmayı bilirim mutlu anlarımda seni.
Yalvaracağım bıkmadan bir sefer daha sana,
aralarında birkaç nefeslik zamanlı sınavlar bu kuluna.

~ * ~

*The tone of the final stanza of “Sınanmak” resembles a call to God. I am, however, not religious and can’t and won’t under any circumstances mislead you in to thinking otherwise. Therefore, please try to see in this poem what I intended to convey: a human being exhausted to her end by the flood of ills that kept coming to her – during an otherwise already utterly trying phase in her life.

To be tested

What to do? It seems impossible at times!

Just when you are about to catch a breath after a trying run;
one more load falls upon these ailing shoulders, quite weak.

The new day demands at times strength to begin afresh;
most souls are left longing for the sun most of the time.

And when then, in a rush, come down
those unbearable weights,
atop this body, already fragile from before…

Although, dimmed eyes fixate on the finishing line,
breath still awaits in hope from the new day's start,
before it is forced to face a fully new ache the heart.

Let it be known:
As does everyone else, I, too, am trying to comprehend
the code of all those unsolvables, ever so eternally present.

While I reproach the reproductive hoop of sorrow,
wondering why this mercilessness never comes to an end.

If I were a believer, I would ask: Have you not known
my patience in face of adversity, my coveting
and my love for you
those sounds of my original self, the child.
My doubts have been ruling over me for long, I know.
If therein lies the reason for your generosity
in your distribution of my sufferings…
Those misgivings
stem from the wandering of the misfortunate mind.

I don't take you for granted during happy times.
Untired of it, I will beg of you one more time.
Let come tests to this mortal of yours
with at least few instances of a break
so that it can take one single fresh breath.

Özlem*

En ufak köşesini bile düşlüyorum bu sıralar memleketin;
o eşsiz kokusu her hücremde, buram buram.
Susamışım inanılmaz.
Doyulacak gibi bir açlık değil bu.
Hasreti dağlamış özünü dimağımın.

Çocukluğum geçti birçok kalp atışında,
hele ki gençliğimin o kaygısız ön yılları;
ilk yetişkinliğimin en ulu cazibesi de orada,
unutamam ne yaşadıklarımı ne de umduklarımı.

Şirin şipşirin bir yeri yokluyor nabzımı vatanın sık sık
denizle kucaklaşmış o masal kitabı gibi şehir

işte o güzelim rıhtım karşıda, çay bahçelerine bakıyor,
can dayımın öğretisi dondurma revanili café ise sağda
iç kıyıdaki hapisane kulesine dürbünle nöbet tutuyor.
Az ötede ada patika, ip incesi,
bir çocuklar bayramı korteji sanki,
ara sokaklardaki hanelerle birlik olmuş coşuyor;
her birinden müzik yüklü yaşantılarımı topluyor.

Ada yolunu izliyorum;
beni en yüksek noktasına götürüyor şehrin;
deniz tüm heybeti ve canlılığıyla göz önünde, sere serpe.

İşte karşımda duruyor o ev, çocukluğumun tüm esrarıyla.
Biraz benzi atmış boyasının,
gene de şatafatlı, o şehrin denizi kadar.
Tarifsiz bir şefkat kokuyor üzerine yayıldığı toprağında.
Pencereler göğe doğru uzanmış iyice sanki,
artık içini ısıtamayan can varlıklarım gibi.

Annemi algılıyorum merdivenlerinde o evin.
Genç. Hayat parlıyor. O kadar da güleç.
Bir de elimdeki geçmişe bakıyorum...

Küçücük bir çocuk o birden,
annesi yanında, pencereden babasını izliyor;
elinde çanta başında pek yakışan geniş kenarlı bir şapka;
yanındaki çocuk o bambaşka can yakınım.
Anneannemi pek seçemiyorum – karanlıkta kalmış.
Annem yanında, dedim, ama peki ya kucağındaki bebek?
O da karanlıkta.
Tamam, tanıdım. Pek az tadabildiğim
o çocuktan hasta diğer can varlığım.

Yanıbaşımda annemin kokusu, kalbinin sımsıcaklığı.

Kah yürüyorum dar dik yokuşlarında o şehrin;
kah dalmış çocuk gözlerim denizine uçsuz bucaksız.
Korumda yaşanmışlıkların yaşanamamışlıkların ağırlığı
yaşanabileceklerin endişesi hem de meraklı bekleyişi.
Bir de şu toprağını içlemesi yok mu şu gurbet ağacının!

Bahara gözyaşları içinde dalları.
Uzun sürdü kış bu sefer.
Güneşine yanık ana vatanın ve de içe çekilesi havasına.

Yanıbaşımda annemin kokusu, kalbinin sımsıcaklığı.

~ * ~

*At first, "Özlem" has been a mere idea for a Turkish to English translation for me. As time passed by, my severe longing for Sinop, Turkey – home to eight generations on my mother side, became a drive in me to compose another poem. While I realize, "Sinopem" – also in *Trance,* is not a translation work, in order to avoid even the slightest repetition of any kind, I am re-introducing it to you in lieu of a literal translation of "Özlem."

~ * ~

Sinopem*

the homeland enters the main vein
her scent floods to each body cell
one stunning aroma after another
i thirst in hunger pangs

etched to memory in blood and flesh
the magic of my early life
often asleep – head should feel sore
however when awake cold or ache no more
blanket soaking in her perfume
pillow, one of softest feathers
"snow falls upon who sleeps" she whispers…

one corner – a distinctive delight
a town in unison with its sea
unlocks the long suppressed

there!
it stretches to the harbor in cheer
main street down tea gardens of yesteryear
Divan café – loyal as ever before
hugs the aged salt factory to affectionately mend
guards before the old prison the compliant inner bay
not at all anxious by its fast descending bend
sates with secrets-devouring treats
my childhood eyes and arousing sighs
on loads and loads of mouth-watering plates
a huge piece of Revani* – apt for my sweet-tooth-fame
topped with natural ice cream of vanilla beans
delights generation after generation after generation
eight in total the loved ones of mine

farther away lies the town's aorta
the legendary passage to famed Ada
coveting April 23rd parades of ribbon bouquets
on Çocuk Bayramı – Festival of Children…
flows in sync with streets wide open alleys unseen
carries along a dear one of mine
to the heart's mind scene by scene

my eyes lock on the trail to the highest peak
one modest look to the left or the right
the sea struts its azure wealth and might

and there a breath away
dons mysteries that spectacular house
bricks worn out shutters ashen hue
still erect in humility though
vies few more breaths to accrue
ornate transoms eye the vastness of the sky
their weathered glances down upon the sea
the soil tender as a new mother's caress
depleted tree roots soon to finally rest
as have those who were put there abreast

my heart wanders off to the faded print:
wide steps to a wooden tall entry door
a stately man – fedora briefcase handsome face
my uncle by his leg – a mere toddler
a Shirley Temple though Turkish – my mother
her tiny gleaming face ever so bright
glued to the colossal front window

my grandmother's beauty in the dark
on her lap my other uncle – her youngest
his cruel damaged pre-natal heart
cut off too soon his contagious delight

next to me
the unique scent of my mother
the warmest warmth of her soul

~ * ~

*Sinop/e of the Turkish Black Sea; "Sinopem: my Sinop; Revani: A traditional Turkish dessert made of semolina and heavy syrup.

Baba…

genç idi oğlun kızın
çok erken öldü annem
az yedin bollukla yedirdin
giydin daha fazlasını giydirdin
gerdin kanadını, kattın annemin kollarına
sevdin annem için sevdin kendince sevdin
biz de sevdik seviyoruz
ama sana ne verebiliyoruz
yer yer acı incitici alaylı ağır sözler
karısından kocasından kızından oğlundan
haksız yere yermeler eleştiriler ve daha niceleri
yoktu ve de hala da yok o çirkin tutumların
tek bir mazereti…

Beni affet.

Dad…

your son was young, your daughter too
my mother died too soon
you ate little but fed in abundance
put on clothes for yourself but gave much more
you spread your wing, extended mom's arms
loved for mom loved in your way
we, too, loved and love
what, however, do we ever give you
hurtful bitter derisive remarks at times
from his wife her husband your daughter your son
unfair villifications accusations and more
there never was nor there is
an excuse for those unseemly behaviors…

Forgive me.

Bir hayat

Hiç sıkmadılar annem ve babam büyütmeye gelince beni.
Desteklediler hep kendime öz güvenimi.

Gene de ben kızlara özgü tek liseye gittim. Kendi seçimim.
Zamanımın ve şehrimizin en iyi lisesi.
Üstün başarıyla bitirdim.
Şaşkın kaldım üniversitemin karşısında –
erkek-kız karışımına.

Ve onunla tanıştım. İlk erkek arkadaşım.
Üniversite yıllarımın yoldaşı.
Kafa dengim. Yetişme dengim. İlgi dengim. Aşk dengim.
Sevdim. Çok sevdim. Hem de pek çok sevdim...

Oysaki tereddütte babam, huzursuz annem.
Başka erkek tanımadın dediler.
Çok genç dediler. Dediler ki şu. Dediler ki bu...
Yas tuttum. Fazlasıyla inatçı bir yas tuttum.
Gene de ayrı kaldım.
Sevdim. Çok sevdim. Hem de pek çok sevdim...

Uygun görülmemişti ya hani o bana.
Avutuldum. Kendi kendimi avuttum.
Algılayamadım o zamanlar ruhumun ikizi olduğunu.
Evlenip yurt dışında mastırımızı yapacaktık.
Burs kazanmıştık da beraber...
Artık ne benden ne ondan bir eser.

Karşı dairemizde aile dostu teyzenin oğlu.
Beni hep severmiş meğer.
İsteyecekmiş çoktan nişan, ben onunla olmasaymışım eğer.
Tanıyoruz birbirimizi çocukluktan.
Bu teyzeye annem, anneme ise bu teyze hayran.
Meğerse şiddetli kapris ve kompleks içinde –
nişan sonrası acı dili, eleştirileri üzerimizde.
Açıldı aralar. Yaratmış meğerse
iki erkek kardeşine de benzeri sorunlar.
Ayrıldım. Onunla evliliği hayal ettim, hem de çok ettim.
Ama olamazdık beraber.

Geçti aradan çok az bir zaman.
Buldu üniversite içinde beni kocam.
Araya koydurmuştu bölümler arasında bir çöpçatan.
O asistan ben asistan.

Annemin rahatsızlığı başladı aniden o günlerde.
Kanser – hem de en kararlılarından öldürmeye.
Denilmişti: romatizma...

İster ki anneciğim kendi evimi bileyim.
Ben o önden gitsin dedikçe,
hükmediyor hastanede yatağından hepimize.
Hükmediyor dediysem, tabii ki iyiliğime kendince.
Endişeli aşırı duygusal ben için.
Korkuyor, ölümden bile belki çok.
Ya kalırsam o ölünce ben sevgisiz ve biteviye buruk...

Acele nişan oluyor. Düğün takip ediyor.
Annem de uygun gördü ya artık.
Ben tedirgin ben ürkek ben gönülsüz.
Burkula burkula özüm, içimdeki fırtınaları sindirmeden yürüyorum nikah masasına. Dans bile ettiriyorlar bana.
Kutlayacak bir şeyim varmış gibi adeta.
Amerika narkoz oluyor bana.
Uzak eskimden, hem de çok uzak.
Bir seneye kalmıyor evliliğim, dönüyoruz Türkiye'ye.
O harika insanımı gömmeye.

Ağabeyim yeni evli. Karşı dairede hala hislendiğim.
Eş ruhum her zaman en derinde.
Niyetleniyorum ifade etmeye
karısına ağabeyime, ısınamadığıma bir türlü bu evliliğe.
Beceremiyorum açıkça demeyi mutsuzluğumu,
durumun benim için umutsuzluğunu.
Kaderim buymuş, diyorum.
Kocamla Amerika'ya geri dönüyorum.

İkinci senenin arifesindeyiz evliliğin.
Yelteniyorum bir hamleye daha.
Ayrılmaya.
Öğreniyorum ki, babam evlenmek üzere.
Ağabeyimin kendi evi var rayına oturtacak.
Diğer can yakınım – dayımın kalabalık ailesi,
üstelik Almanya'da.
Hiç hali olabilir mi kimsenin benim için tasalanacak.

Dönüyorum Amerika'ya geri.
Deniyorum ayrılmayı bir üçüncü kez daha,
dayım ve ailesi ziyarete geldiklerinde beni.
Farkettiği için kocam bendeki soğukluğu,
etmiş dayımdan rica bana düşen sorumluluğu.
Bu sefer doğruyu söylüyorum.
Dobra dobra.
Deyince dayım ama:
kocan iyi çocuk, ne olabilir ki alternatifin?
Kendime güvensizliğe mağlup oluyorum.
O yaz sonunda hamile kalıyorum.

Doğduktan sonra Bir Tanem,
hayat yeniden veriyor kendisini bana.

Geçiyor yıllar. Onlarca yıla katlanıyorlar.
Bir bakıyorum ki, elli olmuş yaşım.
Huzursuzum, mutsuzum evliliğimde.
Kaplamış benliğimi koyu bir kasvet.
Kalamam artık içime ağlaya ağlaya, küse küse hayata,
gülmeye devam ederek dışa
yıllar ve de onyıllar daha boyunca.
Ne olursa olsun sonuç...

Kaldı ki, Bir Tanem –
kendimi seve seve bırakıp kendisine verdiğim
o eşsiz insanım, hayattaki en büyük şükranım
kendi narin ama çetin ayakları üzerinde
öylesine hazır ki artık bulmaya kendi yolunu
germiş güvenle kanatlarını benden uçmaya doğru...

A life

My mother and father raised me with space for my privacy.
Always in support of my own confidence in me.

Nevertheless, I opted for an all-girls' school.
Our city's learning place of high reputation of the time.
I graduated with honors.
College found me surprised – for its male-female blend.

And: I met him. My first boyfriend.
The companion of my undergraduate years.
My mind's equal. Equal to my upbringing.
My partner of hobbies. My love's match.
I loved. Loved much. Loved very much…

My father, however, hesitant; uneasy, my mother.
You haven't known another male, they said.
He is very young, they said.
They said this. They said that…
I mourned. A most determined kind of mourning.
Still, I stayed away.
I loved. Loved much. Loved very much…

He just was not found to be a match.
I was consoled. I consoled myself.
Unaware then of our twinned souls.
Our master's studies were awaiting us abroad.
To follow our wedding.
On scholarships we both had earned…
There was no sign of him or me anymore.

The family friend's son in the flat across from the hall,
had apparently been in love with me all along.

And had been hoping for an engagement for long,
had I not been with him.
We knew each other since childhood.
His mother was in awe for mine;
as mine was a true fan of his.
Once out of her outer shell, she turned acutely whimsical,
suffering from inferiority complexes;
bitter words in abundance, bashing them on our heads,
right after our engagement.
The family friendship was now spoiled.
A fact emerged: in the far past,
her two brothers had to go through her similar issues.
I left him. Imagined marriage with him.
In rigorous images, I imagined marriage with him.
A union had become impossible.

Very little time passed by.
My husband found me at the university.
He had involved the departments for matchmaking.
He was a teaching assistant; so was I.

Ensuing days witnessed my mother ail with a sudden onset.
Cancer – one of the most determined to kill, to boost.
Rheumatism was the initial diagnosis…

I should have a home of my own,
my dear mother wished openly.
He can go ahead, was my reaction. The more I insisted,
the more dominating she became;
concluded it all from her hospital bed for us.
I say, she dominated. Of course, for my sake.
Her concern was vast. For the excessively sensitive me.
She must have feared for me.
Perhaps more than death itself.
What if, her death left me behind
without love and ceaselessly bitter…

Swiftly, the engagement takes place. Wedding ensues.
My mother saw it all to be fit, after all.
I am ill at ease nervous reluctant.
My true self, distorted; internal tremors, not yet quieted.
A walk to the registry table, festivities to follow.
They even have me dance.
As were there something to celebrate.

America sedates me. A far distance from the old; very far.
My marriage passes barely a year. We return to Turkey.
To bury that fantastic being of mine.

A newylwed, my brother. Still there,
the one in the flat across the hall. My soul's twin,
always in the deepest. I attempt to confess.
To my brother. To his wife. Of the cold I feel
in my marriage. I end up incapable.
My unhappiness. My despair.
Hence is my fate, I conclude. And with my husband
come back to America.

We are on the verge of the marriage's second year.
I make another attempt. To divorce.
My father is remarrying, I find out.
He has his own household, my brother;
one he needs to settle down.
My other dear being – my uncle's family is large.
Besides, he is in Germany.
How can anyone worry about me.

I go back to America. Attempt divorce a third time,
when my uncle visits with his family.
Bothered by my cold behavior, it turns out,
my husband approaches him to talk to me,
to demand from me my responsibilities.

I say it as it is this time. Candidly.
'Your husband is a good man,
what could be your alternative?'
Upon hearing my uncle's words,
I succumb to my insecurity.
At the end of that summer, I get pregnant.

After my One and Only is born,
life gives itself to me anew.

Years pass by. Multiply in sets of ten.
One day, as if all of a sudden, I turn fifty.
I am uneasy, unhappy in my marriage.
My inner being is covered in intense gloom.
I see no way to stay on anymore,
while I cry on the inside, quarrel with life
yet keep smiling on the outside,
for years and tens of years more to come.
No matter what the outcome…

Above and beyond,
my matchless being, the biggest blessing of my life
for whom I eagerly pushed myself aside
my One and Only is all ready
to find her own path on her delicate but tough feet
having spread in confidence her wings on her flight…

Susadım Sana

Ayrılığın şaşmaz hükmü
adresimde ezeli nöbette.
Söz dinlemez solumdaki
sana susadı ölesiye.

Yirmi dört saat alt tarafı.
Geçip bitiyor gün ve gece
ama ancak başkasına gelince...
Söz konusu benim, deyince
çörekleniyor hemen kasvet üstüme.
Ne kalp ne beden pes diyor gene de
sana susup duruyor tükenesiye.

Sensizlik gülüp te gülememek.
Kiminle neden bilememek.
Ölmeden tekrar tekrar ölmek.
Sana susayıp susayıp içememek.

Thirsty for You

The infallible sentence on separation
is on eternal guard at my address.
Won't obey, the one on my left side
it violently thirsts for you.

A mere twenty-four hours, it is, after all.
The day and night pass by, and end
but only then, if it were someone else...
As soon as I reveal, it is I,
darkness is swift to twine over me.
Still, neither the heart nor the body gives in
both thirst after you in self-depletion.

Being without you
is to be incapable of laughing when in laughter.
Not to know with whom and why.
To die again and again without having died.
While thirsting after you over and over
not being able to drink you to sate.

Cana Tak Deyince

Rahat bir hayat. Ayrıcalıklı. Oldukça emin.
Kurulmuş düzen. Krokisi çıkmış geleceğin.
Yerleşik ahbaplıklar. Hepsi el altında.
Telaşlar yönelik anlık yaşama, günlük kazançlara.

Diğer tarafta sen…

Sevgin ve sen
Sevgimle sen
Uzaklarından bile beni sevebilmen
Seni ruhumda tenim kadar ben hissettirmen
Ve kaynağına doymayı bilemeyen bir özlem.

At the End of One's Tether

Making a comfortable living in an esteemed life.
Considerably certain.
An order of design. The future's map is out.
Convenient built-in friendships.
Hustle and bustle over immaterial ruts, and daily dimes.

You, on the other hand...

You with your love
You with my love
How you reach me from your distance
How trusted you are to my soul,
as were it inside my own frame.
And my soul with its insatiable pining.

ölümüne aşk

tatmadım böyle bir his bugüne dek
bende şüphe yok, bu başladığı gibi sürecek
eksilmemiş biraz bile uzun zamanlar boyu
yıllar eridikten sonra da öyle devam edecek

coşku hüzün sevinç şüphe özlem ve arzu
henüz adı olmayan nefes kesici daha birçok duygu
kaybetmek duyduğum en büyüklerinden bir korku

ne farkeder beraberlik olmuyorsa eğer

muhtaç değil ki iki tek ruh birleşmesine sevginin
o köklü şefkatin anlayışın ve ilginin

bir kez var olmuşsa doğuştan yek iki tenli bir ruh
önemi yok bir yarının
vücut bulmasına yanında kendi yarımının
çünkü o zaten kendine
kendinin ilk nefesinden daha da yakın

eternal love

this sense, an unknown one from before
no doubt, when it is i who is concerned
this shall last as it began
not lessened for all this time
it will carry on
years can melt one by one

rapture grief joy suspense yearning and desire
breathtaking yet unnamed feelings furthermore
losing, the biggest of the fears i ever did perceive

what difference does lack of a union make

the single two-bodied love is in no need to become one
nor does that affection understanding or desire
donned with deepest roots

once a pre-natal being, though now a dual-bodied soul
the one half can bear not to merge with its other half
for it cannot be possibly closer to itself
than its original breath.

seçimim

farkı mı sevişimin diğer sevenlerden
özün yarısı sevgili ruhu nefese eş beslerken
uzaklardan yakını görmeyenlerden;
tamamlamışsa ikinci bir şans eseri öksüzlüğünü
son anına dek kendini ona vermeyenlerden;
anne karnı öncesi benlik bilirken bu gerçeği,
varmışçasına sanki bir yedeği,
yaşamı adım adım ölüme itenlerden;
henüz yaşantıların bitiş anı gelmemişken
her gün yavaş yavaş ölenlerden?

bütünümle baş koymuşum ben sevgiye,
direnmeye razıyım ten tümden eriyene dek;
bulmuş yarımımı yarımım geç bir mucizeyle,
soldakinin en son atışına dek kendini verecek;
itmeden hayata hasret yaşamımı henüz ölüme,
alabiliyor ki madem o vahadan hala bir nefes
her gün yavaş yavaş ölmeye yatak döşemeyecek.

my choice

the difference between my love and that of those
who overlook the near for the sake of the distance,
while the soul's half feeds its other like its own breath;
who avoid to commit to their rescuer for the second chance,
for relieving them of their orphanage;
who haul life to death step by step, as were there a spare,
when the pre-natal ego knows this truth too well;
who die little by little each day,
although life's end is still far away?

my commitment to love is unbroken,
it is ready to resist until skins decay;
my half found its other with much delay,
though in a most magical way;
it will remain there until the heart beats its last;
while that oasis still inhales to it a fresh breath,
it will not force to die a life that quests to live,
nor will it prepare for it the bed of death.

Ölüme yaşamak*

sensiz gene özlem giyindim bugün
geceye neyse ki var henüz biraz
uğraşıyla gün geçiyor bir şekilde
onun bitişi yok mu ama az ve az...
aynı dirençle
yılmadan
her gün
ten
umutlayıp da kendini
bulabilmeye o tek eşini
iki tek değil de
bulmuyor mu her seferinde bir tek teni

yaşanmış bir şekilde seneler
birçoğu boş dolu bazısı
ya beş ya on belki de yirmi
hiç alacağım kalmışsa geri

beden ruhun pek gerisinde
kopacak tümden yakın günün birinde
arzu etme edilme ihtiyacı
gene de yaşayacak, iste ya da isteme
gün de bitmeyi beceremeyecek
gece hele hiç mi hiç geçemeyecek

sensiz gene özlem giyindim bugün
tutunmaya gayretli anılar bile
o iki benliği ha terketti ha terkedecek
hiç sevmemiş hiç sevilmemişcesine
sanki kalbimde kalbin asla atmamış gibi
bu yarım ruha biteviye özlem yükleyecek

to live for death

my thirst for you dressed me again today
there still is some time til the night sets in
work somewhat helps pass the day
when it nears its end, though, little by little
with the same resistance
steadfast resolve
every single time...
the hope-filled body hungers for its match
to only find its one self instead

the years were lived somehow
many, in grey blur; some color-filled
five ten or maybe even twenty
if any more are left for me, that is

the body lags; the soul is ahead
some day soon, they will be detached
regardless...
the need for desire and to be wanted will survive
the day will not know an end
it will cease to expire, the night

my thirst for you dressed me again today
even resilient memories
are about to forsake those two ids
as if i had never loved nor had ever been loved
as if your heart had never beaten in mine
they will burden anew this unfinished soul with hunger

yanık

yanma kalbim, ne olursun, yanma
senin coşkunla sevgi vermeyenlere
alışkanlığa asıl hayat bu diyenlere
düzenlerinden vazgeçmeyenlere

biliyorum, perişansın, korundan yandın
yoluna git, ne olursun, ancak öyle varsın

durmaz, bilirim, iner ard arda o alev yaşlar
günün birinde herhalde bu acı da yavaşlar
zannetme ki, için acımasız hep böyle kavlar

eş ruhun bildin, sevgiye özünü verdin
göz kamaştıran bir serapmış meğer

yanma kalbim, ne olursun, yanma
matemde kal, başka ne var, sanki ne farkeder
hiçe vardı sevgin, bittin tükendin sanma
günün birinde elbette bu yanık da geçer

the burn

stop the burn, my heart
i beg of you, stop the burn
ignited by those not as generous with love
who see in habitude the real life to live
who refuse to forgo matters of convenience

i know your misere, this deepest of burns
go it alone, i beg of you, go it alone
only then, you will survive

those tears will not end, they are on fire
i think also this ache will ease one day
your essence will surely not keep burning like this

you took him as your soul's twin
and gave your whole self to love
a mere blinding mirage, it seems,
was all that there was

stop the burn, my heart
i beg of you, stop the burn
though keep alive mourning
what else is left, what difference does it make
think not your loving was in vain
believe not you finally died out
some day, also this burn will terminate

Sinop'u sevmek (Pantun*)

ülkemin en alçak gönüllü yöresi
sarmış benliğimi henüz ben doğmadan
denizinin misafirperver köşesi
karşılayacak bedenimi kucaktan

~ * ~

*To avoid repetition, a description of Pantun only shows up in the first section of *Trance* where my poem in English with the title "love gone wrong (Pantun)" appears.

loving Sinop (Pantun)

the most modest piece of my home soil
encompassed my essence before i was born
the hospitable corner of its sea
will welcome my body in warm embrace

epilogue

hülya n. yılmaz

about the Author

hülya yılmaz is a college professor in Liberal Arts with an extensive teaching career. She authored a research book on the influence of ghazal poetry by Rumi and Hafiz on 19th and 20th century German literature. Another scholarly work contains her chapter on a controversial novel by Orhan Pamuk, the 2006 recipient of the Nobel Prize for Literature. From her profession, however, she cherishes most the conduct and words of appreciation from a respectable number of students. In her creative work, yılmaz prefers the genres of fictional autobiography, short story and poetry. Presently, she teaches full-time in her fields of specialty; does creative writing; is a self-appointed literary translator and a novice free-lance writer.

a few words from hülya

Composing poems had been a fascinating exploration for me during my early schooling in Turkey, my country of birth. I remember in vivid images the time when I saw my lyrical creations in the poetry section of a popular journal. The same publisher also printed a short story I had written with the editor's invitation. Decades passed since. While I haven't stopped writing poems or prose, life's demands took over the concentration I used to have back then to pursue my passion for creative work. I was convinced any writing endeavor was no longer meant for me.

About a year and a half ago, I joined the blogging arena. I began to write again with devotion. Most of my written work on my blog needs revising, a process I haven't been able to attend to due to serious time restraints. But, I have been writing with regular intervals – almost regardless of whatever comes my way in terms of unwarranted distraction. During the process, the more my readers responded to my written word, the better I wanted to write for them and for myself. Courage grew in me to submit – though in a very small amount – my work to writers' platforms. Amazing developments that brought me to the verge of *Trance* began to occur soon after – as I shared with you in my acknowledgments.

When I write, I weave my thoughts and emotions between Turkish – my native tongue, English and German – my acquired and professional languages. The English versions of my poems in Turkish and German are my own work in a blend of the idiomatic and literal translation styles. With regard to the genres, I also prefer not to limit myself only to one. Recently, for instance, I finished a short story to which I lent characteristics of a memoir. A novel I have been working on (with no aignificant progress in sight) displays elements of autobiographical fiction. Poetry, however, signifies my most authentic nature. I therefore remain in eternal gratitude to William S. Peters, Sr. and Janet P. Caldwell of Inner Child Press. For they enabled me my trilingual poetic voice to tell my story.

Cultural upbringing, gender issues, parenting, death, sorrow, joy, and the one phenomenon that stabilizes it all – love with its own offerings of longing, elation, loss and mourning, are the themes I attempt to evoke in my book. Words by renowned poets, writers and philosophers announce the emergence of a new set of thoughts, emotions or a union of both. In each of my poems, then, I articulate life experiences we all traverse. Their tone and symbolism vary according to the coping mechanisms that happened to be only my share.

It is my hope for my poetry to reaffirm for you the concept of sameness among us. Whether it is about the written word in one or the other language, we are not at all as different from one another as we may assume to be. For the only distinction lies in the extent to which our identical or similar ordeals and joys have moved and continue to move us toward our own transformations.

As for my passion for the literary genre through which I am privileged to connect with you on whichever level of our existences that may be, I reveal it to you with words from Henry Charles Bukowski (1920-1994):

"Poetry is what happens when nothing else can."

what people are saying . . .

I met hülya n. yılmaz when she joined a private group on Facebook for writers of prose, poets, and artists to donate our talents to anthologies that benefit various charities called *Indies In Action*. I was immediately impressed with her talent as a writer and poetess as well as her vivacious personality and we quickly became friends.

We live in a society where women are often represented as drama queens, needy and clingy, or completely devoid of emotion. hülya's poetry portrays women as warm, caring, and with inner strength that enable them to maintain composure in the face of adversity. It brings to mind all of the best qualities I would like my daughter or granddaughter to have if I had one.

Crystal Schall

Writer, Editor

Professor Hülya N. Yılmaz is yet to showcase her masterpieces in her book "Trance", a poetry book collection in English, Turkish and German. Her poetry encompasses thought-provoking insights of the world around us, intricately written as embedded in her poetry works.

Dr. Yılmaz who considers herself an interrupted writer and poet, armed with her impressive literary achievements and experiences will give her readers lovely-woven words – words of a modern poet who wonders about the miracles and mysticism of life and beyond, weaves them and produces inspirational works about different themes, I am sure you would all fall in love with. Reading her poetry makes me feel as though I am in those moments in time when she had actually composed them. I was asked in an online magazine interview before what is perfect poetry for me. "Perfect poetry for me is one that awakes the feelings of your readers, carries you to a place you have made up in your imagination as written on your pieces, one that touches the readers in one way or the other." That is exactly how I can describe Prof. Yılmaz's poetry.

I highly recommend lovers of poetic works to read "Trance" and experience a different kind of escape out of life's madness for a while and relax enjoying her magnificent poetry.

Congratulations on your new international poetry book, Prof. Hülya N. Yılmaz !

Elizabeth E. Castillo

Writer/Journalist/Blogger
Philippines

What is mind without emotions? What is brilliance without emotions? Worldwide the scientists are hugely focused on the Emotional Quotient (EQ) of humans. Now in *Trance* Dr. hülya yılmaz (Ph.D., Humanities) has silently showcased her strong adherence to the eminent poet William Wordsworth. According to Wordsworth (Ref: *Lyrical Ballads*): "Poetry is the spontaneous overflow of powerful feelings: it takes its origin from emotion recollected in tranquility." With *Trance* the readers will certainly enjoy revisiting memory lane. Poetry has its characteristic spell of silence. In this collection the readers will explore the void of silence. I have thoroughly enjoyed reading the whole of the book but will especially mention the following poems as my most favorite readings: *raising a wife*, *anatomy of a divorce*, *barren no more*, *alive?*, *how?*, *denial*, and *You Are Not Alone*. I believe you, too, will enjoy *Trance* in its entirety, or through the poems of your selection.

Dr. Kiriti Sengupta

November, 2013
Calcutta, India

hülya n. yılmaz, is a woman after mine own heart. I met her in 2013 through a good friend and Author, Alan W. Jankowski. Alan introduced her to one of the many, Inner Child groups of which I not only am a member, but also the COO, of Inner Child, ltd.

I began to read hülya's poetry on a regular basis and found her to be a very capable and versatile writer. This is when my curiosity peaked about this intellectual woman. I was driven to know more. hülya is not only a talented writer but also speaks, writes and teaches in many languages thereby empowering her readers. I personally find intelligence refreshing. hülya is at the top of my list.

I also want to mention that hülya is personable, trustworthy and a lover of mankind, expressing peace and love, for all of humanity; and now a personal friend that I love and adore. Within the pages of *Trance*, you the reader, will see exactly what I mean. hülya, has a way of weaving her poetry into the form of story telling, satiated . . . while leaving you wanting more. Conundrum ? Thank Goodness, I am able to turn the page and read more from this gifted writer. hülya has graciously gifted us with the English, German and her native tongue Turkish, in the translations found within this book, Trance.

Trance is a *steal* at $ 22.95 and I encourage you to buy one for yourself and to gift another. Happy Reading !

Janet P. Caldwell

Author
COO, Inner Child, ltd.
http://www.janetcaldwell.com/

about the Artist

Siddartha Beth Pierce

Siddartha Beth Pierce

Siddartha Beth Pierce is a Mother, Poet, Artist, Educator and Art Historian. Her works are informed by Nature, Math, Science, the Universal, Sub-Conscious and Metaphysical aspects we encounter throughout our lives. She works with a variety of media including painting, drawing, printmaking, sculpture and some computer graphics.

Siddartha says her purpose is one of self-exploration and philosophical research. Her objective is to reach you, the reader and viewer in order to illicit a response mechanism within you own circle of knowledge, heart and soul. She has hope that each of person may find something of value to consider and expand upon their own lives and experiences.

She further says "It is my mission to bring these works to the public at a minimal of expense but with a depth that is far reaching".

Most of Siddartha's works are a part of her own private collection, however, she does welcome any inquiries for the purchase of any art you may be interested in. She has shown my work nationally and has been and is currently featured in print magazines and journals internationally.

She thanks all for taking the time to view and explore this creation.

l'enfant

a few words from the Artist . . .

The cover art for this book was created in 1995 while I attended George Mason University in Fairfax, Virginia. It is a collagraph printmaking plate made of caulk painted with a palette knife onto canvas board. It is a one of a kind artwork. 'L'Enfant: A Foreshadow' is titled as such due to the breech, C-Section birth of my son, Pierce Emery Haver, three years later. I later attended Virginia Commonwealth University in Richmond, Virginia and received a Masters Degree in Art Education with an emphasis on printmaking and computer art and furthered my studies there in the Art History Department. I am now All But Dissertation (ABD) in a degree of Philosophy of Art History with a major in African Art History and Contemporary Art.

Additionally, I was an Assistant Professor and Artist-in-Residence at Virginia State University in Petersburg, Virginia during 2001. Wherein my art, poetry and teaching were featured on PBS, Around the Appomatox.

Siddartha Beth Pierce

Inner Child Press

Inner Child Press is a Publishing Company Founded and Operated by Writers. Our personal publishing experiences provides us an intimate understanding of the sometimes daunting challenges Writers, New and Seasoned may face in the Business of Publishing and Marketing their Creative "Written Work".

For more Information

Inner Child Press

www.innerchildpress.com

intouch@innerchildpress.com

Made in the USA
Charleston, SC
10 January 2014